MW00386590

Egypt at Highclere

The Path to the Discovery of Tutankhamun

CONTENTS

1325BC. Tutankhamun is buried.

1922AD. The 5th Earl of Carnarvon
discovers Tutankhamun's tomb.

1987AD. Lord Carnarvon's Collection of
Egyptian artefacts was famously discovered
by the 6th Earl's butler, hidden in secret
cupboards in Highclere Castle, Newbury.

2009AD. The 8th Earl and Countess open a
new presentation of the Antiquities
Collection and a new Discovery and
Treasures Exhibition, to tell the story of
how the 5th Earl and Howard Carter made
the most important find in archaeological
history: the discovery of the Tomb of
Tutankhamun.

E gyptian civilisation can be traced through a history of over 5,000 years, and still fascinates us today some 2,000 years after its demise. There remain obvious architectural achievements, elegant scripts, complex beliefs, paintings, monuments and art.

The ancient Egyptians seemed to have a sense of who they were, where they came from and where they were going, which is confirmed in their temples, images and writings.

The stability of the culture was determined firstly by geography and, secondly, by organisational skills.

Egyptian culture grew along the River Nile basin which provided fresh water, a very fertile agricultural landscape and was protected by the far stretching inhospitable deserts.

The administration was historically divided into two: the Delta area or Lower Egypt, and the valley of Upper Egypt. The river provided the means of transport between the two regions.

The flooding and retreat of the Nile consistently provided a broad range of crops: from wheat, lentils, cucumbers, hops, vines and flax papyrus to sufficient foods for cattle, sheep and pigs.

The Egyptian year was divided into three seasons: the time of the flood, the time to sow and the time to harvest.

Some of the Egyptian ideas seem very familiar yet others totally alien. The dignity and compassion which characterise much of their art and writings, however, touch our thoughts and behaviour today.

The Egyptians' religion was focused on harmony, on the struggle to create and maintain order as opposed to chaos. Not merely was there a struggle here on earth, but also in the Afterlife, the gods not being immune from their own trials.

The Egyptians painted scenes in their tombs about human morality and one of the most famous allusions is a key theme: each person's deeds and life are finely balanced against a feather of truth, in the presence of a goddess symbolising a universal justice, truth and order. Each person had a fine chance of entering the afterlife.

We know about their beliefs and world because their language was preserved in hieroglyphs. Sadly, we cannot hear" their language today and, like other languages, it was written without vowels, so we can only guess the sounds and poetry.

Above, wall carved images from the tomb of Ramoses, Thebes. (8th Earl, 2006).

Their script, however, really originated in drawing and an Egyptian scribe was firstly a draughtsman and secondly a scribe. One of the key people in this adventure story was firstly a draughtsman and secondly an Egyptologist.

The other key person was firstly an art collector, recognising the Ancient Egyptians' exquisite craft and touch and, secondly, an Egyptologist.

Today, we study history to inform us where and why we are here and where we might be going. Egypt lies at the centre of cultures that now extend towards Europe and the Middle East, and the writings, languages and religion many follow today developed with at least some influence from Ancient Egypt.

No true idea of the real grandeur of Egyptian art can be formed except by visiting the country. Perhaps, however, some of the beauty and passion of the art can be understood and explored through the work of long dead craftsmen and artists in modern day museums.

The Egyptians were a very practical people and much of the art we can still see today is about the everyday things they used.

Their enduring works of art are, howeve complex and represent symbols an aspects of their religious beliefs. Thes beliefs underpinned their acts and deed in this world, as they looked forward t the next.

Most Egyptian art remaining today wa found in their tombs because they wer built from stone, and their houses wer built only from mud.

The tomb was called the house of ete nity where life was eternal, whereas lif in the mud brick house was transient an marked by death.

Captions, pages 4-7

Scenes from the River Nile, Middle Egypt taken on the 8th Earl's expedition, 200?

Above & above right. The Pyramids an Sphinx at Giza and oxen plough photographed by the 5th Earl in 191?

Today, ancient Egyptian history begins with the Pharaoh Narmer (3100BC), simply because he is the earliest historical king for whom we have a written record.

Each Pharaoh had 5 Royal names, but Manetho was not always consistent. His list of Pharaohs was researched from records, most of which do not exist today, some 2,000 years after Manetho's death. (See Pharaonic Dynasties on page 92).

Traces of human settlement date human activity in Egypt to 200,000BC near present day Abydos. The Neolithic cultures are generally called pre-dynastic by Egyptologists, as they pre-date the known list of Pharaohs.

During this time, more animals were domesticated and farmers better understood how to make good use of the fertile flood plains of the Nile. Improving climatic changes began to support larger numbers of people.

The first written Egyptian time-line was constructed by a Greek historian, Manetho of Sebennytos in 300BC. He wrote, in Greek, the 'Aegyptiaca', a collection of three books about the history of ancient Egypt, which divided over 150 Pharaonic kings into 30 dynasties.

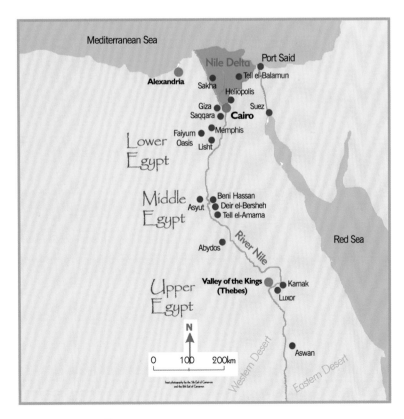

From England to Egypt

The 5th Earl of Carnarvon

Highclere Castle, Newbury

The two men at the heart of the story were both Englishmen, from two very different backgrounds. They became lifelong friends and spent much of their life, not in England, but in Egypt.

George Edward Stanhope Molyneaux Herbert was born in London in 1866. He was the son and heir to the Estates and Earldom of Carnarvon.

His father, the 4th Earl, was a highly respected politician who held various ministerial posts under Conservative Prime Ministers such as Lord Derby and Lord Salisbury.

The 4th Earl travelled both through the exigencies of business as Colonial Secretary and through a love of travel. His son, who became the 5th Earl, inherited his father's interest in travel and exploration.

The 5th Earl of Carnarvon inherited Highclere Castle in 1891, following his father's death.

In 1895, he married Almina Wombwell. Thereafter, he turned his attention to less far flung travels and began to develop more interests at home.

For example, he imported and drove th earliest motor cars, created a Horse Stu in the hills behind the Castle, encourage Geoffrey de Havilland to make his firs aeroplane flight from the Estate, took u photography, and built a golf course.

Following a series of car crashes (in on of which he nearly died), Carnarvon wa advised by his doctors to spend winter in a warm climate well away from th chill and dampnes of England. H decided to go t Egypt.

He had first visite Egypt with his wif as a tourist in 1898 In 1905, he decide to spend 3 month there and to appl for a concession t excavate in Thebes.

He was allotted very unprepossess ing and unpromisin site on some rubbish mounds at Sheik abd el Gurneh, nea the Valley of th Nobles in Thebes.

Each day, he organised his workforce an sat out in the desert closely supervisin them. At the end, he found nothing but mummified cat case.

Undeterred, he returned the followin year and managed to negotiate a bette site. He returned every year, excep during the Great War years, for the nex 17 years.

The 5th Earl of Carnarvon, aged 25

Mr Howard Carter

Ancient wall carving of the Aten Sun disc, near the Valley of the Kings, Luxor

Howard Carter was born in Kensington, London in 1874, the youngest of 11 children. He was a sickly child and spent much of his childhood with his two maiden aunts in Swaffham, Norfolk.

He inherited his father's skills as a draughtsman and, at just 17 years old, left England for Egypt to work as an archaeological draughtsman with, firstly, Percy Newberry and, secondly, the pre-eminent archaeologist of the time: Sir William Flinders Petrie.

Petrie was a difficult and meticulous taskmaster but a matchless mentor. He taught Carter to observe, and to use seemingly irrelevant trifles to deduce historical facts.

1899 was a turning point in Carter's life. The Antiquities Service in Egypt offered him the post of Inspector-in Chief for Upper Egypt and Nubia, with headquarters and a house at Luxor.

The appointment was a tremendous recognition of Carter's qualities and the respect with which his peers held him. Over the next 5 years, he became increasingly well known and experienced.

A disastrous incident in 1905 concerning some rowdy French tourists at Saqqara (near Cairo) turned his world upside down and led to his resignation from the Antiquities Service. He now had no income and nowhere to live and the following two years marked a very low point in his life. He stayed in Luxor and earned an intermittent living from his skills as a draughtsman and water-colourist.

Howard Carter

Nobody knows exactly how and when Carnarvon and Carter met. It may have been through the good offices of mutual friends, or simply through meeting casually in the bar of the Winter Palace hotel in Luxor, where most of the affluent visitors stayed.

Their subsequent collaboration, however, lasted for some 17 years, leading to the most famous archaeological discovery yet recorded. Carter became Carnarvon's man in Luxor, a partner with technical expertise and a meticulous eye for detail and organisation. Carnarvon agreed a salary for Carter and helped him build a house in Thebes, 'Castle Carter'.

'Five Years at Thebes'

Over the next 5 years, they planned their campaigns at Thebes with great precision and care. Carnarvon was able to finance several teams of boys and men working concurrently. They worked around Queen Hatshepsut's Valley Temple, along the Birabi desert edge, and along the cliff face north east of Queen's Hatshepsut's Temple.

They made some remarkable discoveries, such as coffins, statuettes, a gaming board, workman's hoe, necklaces, coins, pottery and papyri.

Carnarvon also bought some beautiful pieces and, thus, created an outstanding collection of Egyptian antiquities which he displayed at Highclere Castle. They published their finds in a book: 'Five Years at Thebes, a record of work done by the Earl of Carnarvon and Howard Carter'.

In June 1914, the American Theodore Davis gave up his concession to the Valley of the Kings. He was 75 years old, his health was failing and he believed that there was nothing more to find:
'I Fear that the Valley of the Kings is now exhausted'.

FIVE YEARS'
EXPLORATIONS AT THEBES

A RECORD OF WORK DONE 1907–1911

BY

THE EARL OF CARNARVON
AND
HOWARD CARTER

WITH CHAPTERS BY

F. LL. GRIFFITH, GEORGE LEGRAIN, GEORGE MÖLLER
PERCY E. NEWBERRY AND WILHELM SPIEGELBERG

WITH SEVENTY-NINE PLATES AND FRONTISPIECE

HENRY FROWDE
OXFORD UNIVERSITY PRESS
LONDON, NEW YORK, TORONTO AND MELBOURNE
1912

six feet long, five feet deep and four feet wide. It had contained jars full of strips of linen rag, natron, broken jars, ointments, floral wreaths and the remains of a meal. These items had been used in the ritual of a burial and, therefore, also received a burial.

Some of the items had the name Tutankhamun on them. Davis decided this was the tomb of Tutankhamun and of no further interest, so he sent the

PREFACE

THE following volume contains a record of work done in the Theban Necropolis during the years 1907–11. In the editing of this report I have availed myself of the generous help of several scholars, whose names appear at the heads of the chapters they have contributed. To these gentlemen I wish to tender my sincere thanks for their co-operation.

Mr. Howard Carter has been in charge of all operations; and whatever successes have resulted from our labours are due to his unremitting watchfulness and care in systematically recording, drawing, and photographing everything as it came to light.

To Professor Sir Gaston Maspero, the Director-General of the Service des Antiquités, I wish to proffer my thanks for his most kind and valuable support; as also to Mr. Weigall, who, in the course of his official work, has given me his most willing assistance. To Dr. Budge I should also like to express my indebtedness for several valuable suggestions.

CARNARVON.

HIGHCLERE,
August 1911.

Carnarvon finally managed to acquire the concession to excavate there. He had longed to work in The Valley of the Kings and believed that there was at least one more tomb to find.

Some years earlier, in January 1908, Theodore Davis had found a pit

items to the Metropolitan Museum New York, where a young curato Herbert Winlock, examined them. realised that they were the embalme cache from the burial of Tutankhamun king about whom little was know Neither his body nor tomb had ever be found.

There had been other clues to the actu existence of a Pharaoh calle Tutankhamun. He was listed as part the 18th Dynasty by the Greek historia Manetho. 1906, a small blu faience cup wi Tutankhamun cartouche on had been found a cache in th Valley of th Kings. A yea later, Davis ha found a cache embalming mat rial, broken po tery and wreaths

Two years late another sma cache had bee found just north Horemheb's tomb, which contained shabti and some sheets of gold, agai with the cartouche of Tutankhamun an his wife Ankhesenamun.

The season for archaeological excavation in Egypt was very short, due to the extreme heat in summer months. The two men often returned to England together in March each year.

Lord Carnarvon led a busy life in England, with diverse interests and responsibilities at his Highclere Castle Estate.

Howard Carter would return to London and Norfolk to visit friends and family, as well as visiting Lord Carnarvon at the Castle.

The following pages explore the various aspects of life for the two men in England in Edwardian times.

...e Chief Keeper of Antiquities at the ...ritish Museum in London was a regular ...sitor to Highclere Castle and in his own ...oks noted discussions with Lord ...rnarvon about Tutankhamun. The

of two priestesses of Amun. Lord Carnarvon had made notes from it trying to identify the location of the tombs.

However, a few months later came the outbreak of the Great War and Carnarvon returned to England to offer his services to the War effort. Carter remained in Egypt and reported for duty to Cairo.

Little further archaeo-logical progress was made in the next few years. Lord Carnarvon was only able to return to Egypt in 1919, after the cessation of hostili-ties.

...ritish Museum owned the Papyrus ...bbott, an ancient Egyptian document ...amed after the original owner, Dr ...bbott, which had been purchased by ...e British Museum in 1857.

...detailed the investigations, by Ancient ...gyptian officials, into tomb robberies ...at occurred during the reign of the ...haraoh, Ramesses IX. Ten Royal tombs ...vere looted, as well as the sanctuaries

3

Motor Carnarvon

Lord Carnarvon was one of the earliest drivers in England and nicknamed "Motor Carnarvon". He was renowned for being a fast and fearless driver and incurred numerous speeding fines.

This page below and page 13, top right. These rare photographs, taken by the 5th Earl of Carnarvon, record his visit to the Dieppe Grand Prix on 2nd July 1907.

Above. Visitors arriving at Highclere Castle, 1910.

He first held a French driving license, as motor car enthusiasts were able to drive in France at greater speeds and with fewer restrictions. In England, for example, a man had to walk in front of a motor car waving a red flag! Reportedly, locals living in Highclere used to tell their children that, if they misbehaved, the man in the big black car with the red flag would take them away.

Much of Lord Carnarvon's driving career can be traced through the speeding fines. The first one was incurred in 1898 in Newbury, when he was summonsed for driving over 12 miles an hour.

A year later, in May 1900, he was summonsed for speeding in Epping. Fortunately, a barrister, Mr. Staple Firth, already specialised at defending motorists and was able to get each case dismissed.

In July 1901, in Epping it was more serious and a policeman described him as coming at a terrific speed dashing down a hill at almost 25 miles an hour. Moreover, neither the Earl nor his mechanic following in a second car stopped when he put

his hand up. Sometimes his chauffeur, M Edward Trotman, was also summonse He had his license suspended for months in 1909.

Lord Carnarvon owned and drove variety of cars, both English and Frenc but his first car was probably a Panhar Levassor in which he toured the connent with his wife, Lady Almina ar French chauffeur, Georges Eilersgaard, 1898. It was left hand drive, had 4 gear and would go at 4½, 7, 10 or 13 miles pe hour.

During the 1890's, the French pioneere the development of motoring. They wer able to use the Daimler engine, which ha been developed in Germany, to the advantage. A Frenchman, Louis Renaul mounted an engine on a de Dio Quadriclye in 1898 and invented the firs shaft drive transmission. Previous ve sions used chains to provide the driv train.

Lord Carnarvon was clearly well verse with all such advances and bought a d Dion Quadricycle himself which he late onated to the Motor Museum in 1912. It as the first car with wheel steering. He mported it into England and it was one of e first petrol driven cars in the UK.

e remained loyal to the French marques. The Societe Anonime Paris ournier holds a bill addressed to Lord arnarvon in 1904 for French Francs 572.80. They were agents for the anhard Levassor.

e also bought an Endurance motor car, uilt in Coventry.

y 1909, Lord Carnarvon had acquired a 8hp Metallurgique (a Belgian make very opular in the UK, where some beautilly styled models appeared between 906 and 1914). He was to be found riving it around Paris and, on August 2th 1909, set off for Constantinople.

ord Carnarvon had some very bad car rashes, the most serious of which was in chwalbach in Germany. He was driving ast along a straight road, with a hidden ip which obscured a bullock cart. Trying o avoid it, he overturned the car.

His chauffeur Trotman was thrown clear but Carnarvon was trapped, pinned underneath the overturned car. He had stopped breathing but Trotman revived him and took him to Schwalbach, where his wife was staying.

He had damaged his head, jaw and lungs and suffered terrible migraines over the next five years. His wife, Almina, nursed him and discovered her own passion which she pursued for much of her life: nursing and medical treatment.

Nevertheless, he remained an enthusiastic car driver with a penchant for speed,

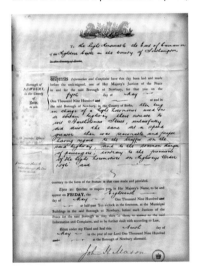

and bought a Bugatti in 1912 and toured France in it.

The speeding fines continued and the fines increased. For example, he paid £2 at Stratford for exceeding the speed limit while motoring in Epping New Road, Loughton, in 1917

Left. Lord Carnarvon's French driving permit.

Below left. Lord Carnarvon's Newbury Court Summons for speeding.

Below. The 5th Earl's grandson, later the 7th Earl, driving his model car, the 'Red Bug', at Highclere Castle in the 1930s.

His health had suffered as a result of the motoring accidents and he was advised to seek warmer climes during the cold, damp English winters.

He chose to go to Egypt, which he had first visited as tourist in 1898.

He had known Sir William Garstin for some years, who worked for the Foreign Office as Director of Irrigation and Public Works in Egypt. One of the departments within this office was that of Department of Antiquities. The connection was useful when obtaining his first concession to excavate at Thebes.

Photographer

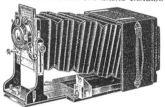

The SINCLAIR "UNA" CAMERA
THE ONLY PERFECT UNIVERSAL CAMERA.

Showing Standard "Una" with Long Extension and the Double Rising Front

The Sinclair "UNA" Camera is THE BEST of its Class,

BECAUSE—

IT is suitable for every class of work.
IT will take short, medium or long-focus lenses.
IT may be fitted with any shutter.
IT has great latitude in all movements.
IT is constructed on practical and scientific lines.
IT has a very great rising front.
IT has a central swing front.
IT has a revolving back.
IT is simple in construction and use.
IT is suitable for Telephoto work.
IT can be fitted with any Changing Arrangement, Dark Slide,
    Changing Box, Eastman Roll Holder or Premo Film Pack.
IT is made of the best materials and with the perfection of workmanship.

JAMES A. SINCLAIR & Co., Ltd., 54, Haymarket, LONDON, S.

Below. Lord Carnarvon's actual camera, which he took on all his expeditions to Egypt from 1905 to 1923.

Lord Carnarvon was interested in new technology and became not only an enthusiastic, but a professional and respected photographer. He was asked to be President of the Camera Club in 1916. Later, he became a pioneer of colour photography.

The camera on display at Highclere was made by James Sinclair of London. They made three types of 'Una' camera, all noted for the quality of their workmanship. Carnarvon used the 'Tropical Una', made from Spanish mahogany with brass bindings, which was able to withstand hot and dry climates.

It is a beautiful camera to look at and was made with great attention to detail in terms of construction and performance.

Lord Carnarvon devoted effort and care to setting up and developing photographs during his travels and excavations in Egypt.

Over 600 photographs provide an extraordinary record of the time, of Egypt and his efforts.

They are all in black and white and half tones although he later began to pioneer colour photography.

The first colour photograph was taken by a Scotsman, James Clerk Maxwell. But, during the early twentieth century, the Lumiere brothers in France experi-

mented with the Autochrome process. required different plates and solution and was even more complex than black and white images. Colour photograph really took off after 1935.

The Adelphi Camera Club held an exhibition of photographs by Lord Carnarvon July 1916. Most of the pictures were of beautiful women but there was also a striking portrait of Lord Ripon holding an ancient vase in his hands entitled "The Connoisseur."

Two months later, his work was exhibited at the Gallery of The Royal Society Pall Mall East, International Exhibition of the London Salon of Photography. Of the portraits it was said that "nothing better could be desired than those shown by Lord Carnarvon".

ord Carnarvon eated a darkroom d studio at the ack of the Castle. It ould not have een completely ack he used a safe mber coloured ht in which to ork. He would also ave to load his imera in dark- ss.

any of Lord rnarvon's photo- aphs are small rmat, as he only ose to enlarge his election for exhibi- ons, making the rocess more ficient.

19 August 1918

"Head study"
1 July 1918

international khibition of Studies in Photography was eld at the Royal Society of Painters, Pall

selection of photographs taken by the h Earl in 1918.

Mall East, on 9th September 1921. The Earl exhibited a Portrait of a Child.

Records suggest Lord Carnarvon photographed a lot of naked women. The pictures were, apparently, tactfully destroyed by his butler after his death.

During the First World War, he was asked to advise the Royal Flying Corp HQ on aerial photog- raphy. The Flying Corp was formed in 1912 and was air support for the Army, providing photographic reconnaissance.

Later, the Corp was involved in strategic bombing of German airfields and transport. Initially, it had 12 balloons and 36 planes. In 1918, it was amal- gamated with the Royal Naval Air force to become the Royal Air Force.

"An English girl",
July 1918

"An important sector of the Hindenburg defences, as seen at 8,000 ft. Showing series of elaborate trenches"

Carnarvon in Egypt

Lord Carnarvon possessed a restle
intellect and a desire to pursue ne
avenues. He decided to apply for a co
cession to excavate at Luxor, some 4c
miles south of Cairo, while staying there

More people were now able to travel, y
it did take considerable organisation ar
time. The trip would involve a boat cros

Lord Carnarvon made the trip from
Southampton to Alexandria sometimes
via Gibraltar and Algiers and also via
Marseille, France and Genoa, Italy.

E gypt had become a well known
tourist destination for the English
during the nineteenth century. However,
travellers had brought back watercol-
ours and tales of extraordinary buildings
and temples for hundreds of years.

Napoleon had included a retinue of over
100 academics in his military expedition
to Egypt in 1801. The European world
became fired up by the promise of hidden treasures and a lost civilization. The
next one hundred years was marked by
various European excavators working
throughout Egypt.

Towards the end of the nineteenth
century the areas of excavation, (conces-
sions), were regulated by a department
of the Egyptian Government, the
Department of Antiquities, which was led
by an outstanding French Egyptologist,
M. Gaston Maspero.

Universities, Egyptian Exploration
Societies and private individuals could
apply for a concession. It was, however,
an expensive process.

Shepheard's Hotel, Cair

ing from Southampton to France fo
lowed by a train journey south to th
Riviera. Lord Carnarvon often sailed fro
Marseille to Alexandria, and then too
the train to Cairo.

He often stayed in Shepheard's Hotel c
the banks of the Nile in Cairo, whic
hosted a truly eclectic gathering o
people: artists, sportsmen, statesme
collectors, invalids and tourists. Like ar
other tourist, he visited the 'souks
Egypt's street markets, the Nile and th
desert, taking photographs as he tra
elled.

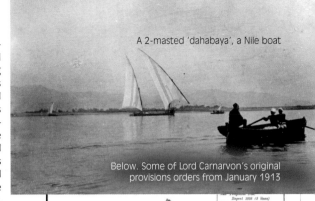

A 2-masted 'dahabaya', a Nile boat

he air in Egypt is clear and dry with no umidity. The evenings are cool, with wift sunsets.

It was and is an easy place to live and Lord Carnarvon began to regain his health. He was accompanied by his doctor, Doctor Johnnie, taking his medicine chest wherever he went. Lord Carnarvon usually travelled by train from Cairo to Luxor, a journey of 12 hours in a comfortable well provisioned railway carriage.

ord Carnarvon first stayed at the Winter Place Hotel in Luxor in 1905. It was an elegant structure, built by the French, with sweeping staircases and large high ceiling rooms. French rugs were scattered across parquet floors and glorious chandeliers hung from the ceilings. Angled white sun blinds shaded the tall windows from the sun during the day. The gardens behind were well watered and full of bougainvillea, hibiscus and palms. Groups of umbrellas were dotted through the gardens for guests to sit well shaded.

Not all the expeditions could be based in Luxor or Cairo. In 1912, Carter and Carnarvon decided to test a Nile Delta site and Carnarvon applied for a concession at Sakha. The Delta sites were much more inhospitable, requiring the Carnarvons, Carter and staff, including Dr Johnnie, to live in tents amongst snakes in thoroughly uninspiring and humid, desolate, muddy hills.

It was a depressing and unproductive place. In 1912, however, they applied to excavate at Tell el-Balamun, another Delta site. This lies 20 km south of the Mediterranean and the muddy fields cover the remains of a temple, a town and a necropolis.

They also sailed on a dahabaya from Luxor to El Minya to plan to work at Tell el-Amarna but, just as they were considering where to excavate next, Theodore Davis, the American archaeologist, gave up his concession to the Valley of the Kings. Lord Carnarvon applied for a concession and, thanks to his diligent past excavations and professional recording thereof, his application was successful.

Below. Some of Lord Carnarvon's original provisions orders from January 1913

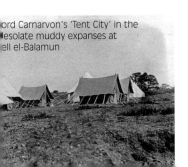

ord Carnarvon's 'Tent City' in the esolate muddy expanses at ell el-Balamun

Carnarvon at Highclere

Lord Carnarvon, above far left, established a golf course on the Highclere Estate

The 5th Earl inherited a love of farming and the countryside from his father, who farmed wheat and barley, bred rare pigs as well as sheep and, like his father, entered his livestock for shows throughout his life.

Horse Racing

In 1896, however, he began a new interest: horse racing, registering his colours of Eton Blue and Black.

Part of his wife's family had a passion for racing, as did many of his friends. In 1899, he bought a horse called Simonside for 1,100 Guineas, which won the 2,000 Guineas at Newmarket.

He bought further horses such as Baldur, St Colon, Dark Daniel, Kunstler and The Solicitor.

The Highclere Stud

He decided to create a Stud at Highclere using a grassy bowl of some 250 acres in the hills behind Highclere Castle, between Beacon Hill and Siddown Hill. He bred and raced noted thoroughbreds for the next 20 years.

He was a leading figure at the newly built Newbury racecourse which opened on September 26th 1905. His horses won three races on the first day. 1909 was a most successful racing year with

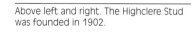

Above left and right. The Highclere Stud was founded in 1902.

18

noted horses such as Bembo, Malpas and Valens. They ran in races at Epsom, Newbury and Newmarket.

He owned a useful filly called Wassillissa, which was second in the Oaks in 1914. He sometimes achieved excellent sale prices after the Great War, but only had one really useful horse, Franklin, who won consistently in 1921.

His horses came first in the Hardwicke Stakes at Ascot, second in the St. Leger and first at Newmarket in October of that year and repeated the Newmarket success in the following year.

In 1919, he became a member of the Jockey Club and was a founder member of the Thoroughbred Breeders Association.

AT THE EPSOM SPRING MEETING: "THE CITY AND SUBURBAN"

Lord Carnarvon's Horse, "Robert le Diable," Winning the City and Suburban

Another cloudless day brought more people to Epsom than the day before. His Majesty, accompanied by Prince Christian, went down to Epsom to see this popular race run. "Robert le Diable" (W. Lane up), won a good race by three lengths, Mr. J. B. Joel's "Dean Swift" taking second place, and Lord Westbury's "Cerisier" third

Shooting

Lord Carnarvon was one of the best shots in the country. Shoots at Highclere were renowned for the quality and quantity of game. The shoot books record bags of rabbits, pheasant and partridge shot by famous guns such as Lord de Grey, Lord Ashburton, the Duke of Marlborough, Prince Dhuleep Singh and Prince Albert (later King Edward VII).

AT KEMPTON ON SATURDAY.

Lord Carnarvon (wearing a white hat), at Kempton Park on Saturday. His horse, Abelard, was second in the May Auction Plate, won by Lady Dainty.

The Prince of Wales visited Highclere in December 1895. He is seen here, middle back row holding a cane.

The Castle at War

Highclere Castle Visitor books bear witness to the statesmen, writers, Royalty, Egyptologists, journalists, friends and relations who came to stay. Often, they gathered together for race meetings at Newbury Racecourse.

After shooting parties, or games of golf, evenings were spent re-assessing the 5th Earl's latest Egyptian acquisitions, debates in the House of Lords or local matters of concern.

The Castle, however, was about to take on a very different role. In July 1914, General Kitchener came to have lunch with the Earl and Countess of Carnarvon at Highclere Castle. Almina presented a proposal to the General. She wished to turn the Castle into a hospital for wounded officers.

Even without the benefit of hindsight, it was clear Europe was tumbling into war. No-one could guess the future devastating loss of life at that point.

Almina wanted Army and medical approval for the conversion, should it be necessary for the Castle to be requisitioned.

So, later that year, the first wounded soldiers were driven up from Southampton to Highclere, a bumpy journey taking some two hours. Sometimes, Lady Carnarvon would go and collect the soldiers herself and drive them back.

She enjoyed the actual nursing and had trained part-time in a London hospital over the previous two years. She also watched and helped in operations. The bedrooms were turned into dormitories. Arundel Bedroom was converted into an operating theatre. She employed a resident doctor, a radiologist and a team of some 30 nurses, dressing the nurses in uniforms of fuchsia and white.

She fed her occupants very well. She paid for specialists to travel from London to help some patients, many of whom had dysentery as well as gunshot wounds. Comfortable chairs, good beer and a whisky at night all contributed to a successful recovery. Patients were moved

Arundel bedroom, which was used as an operating theatre during the Great War

It was decided that Aubrey should go to London to stay with his sister, Lady Victoria Herbert, in Stratford Place. Aubrey commented how well he was treated by the Germans and was very appreciative of their care.

In 1916, Almina transferred her hospital to London to set up in Portland Place. Highclere returned to a skeleton staff

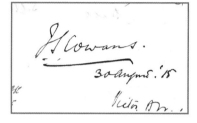

on after two or three months to make room for new cases.

Lord Carnarvon was 48 years old and not in good health. He volunteered to help organise and advise the Royal Flying Corp on aerial photography. His younger half brother, Aubrey Herbert, however, had signed up and joined the War effort.

In September 1914, Aubrey was posted as missing in action. He was an MP for Yeovil and had joined the Special Reserve Corps as an interpreter, attached to the Irish Guards. He had appalling eye sight. On September 7th, he was sent to fetch a message and fell wounded.

Like all soldiers, he had been given three morphine pills, one of which he was told to take *in extremis*. Believing that he was going to die, he took all three pills, which knocked him out and slowed all internal bleeding. Later, he was collected as one of dead by the Germans. Startling one of his captors, he was transferred to a German Field hospital, where they dressed his wounds. Shortly afterwards, an Allied advance took over the German Field Hospital.

Meanwhile, hearing the news, Lord Carnarvon arranged to go to France to make a personal search for his brother, finding him in the newly acquired Field Hospital.

and sometime residence for the Carnarvon family until the War ended.

Lord Carnarvon's son, Lord Porchester, later the 6th Earl, enlisted in 1915 at the age of 17, and sailed to join his Regiment in Meerut, just north of Delhi.

In October 1917, he was sent with his Regiment into Mesopotamia, now Iraq. He had various lucky escapes and, by the close of the Campaign, half of his Regiment had been killed in action or died from disease.

He returned to London in the Spring of 1919.

The War Years at Highclere Castle. Right, one of Lady Carnarvon's nursing staff. Left and above, wounded soldiers recuperating. The extract from the Visitor Book on this page includes the signature of Lt.Gen. J. Cowans, Quarter Master General of the British Army, during his visit on 30th August 1915.

Post War

On 31st January 1918, Lord Carnarvon was taken ill after lunch and travelled to London for treatment. He was seriously ill and was operated on for appendicitis. He was later nursed back to health by his wife and daughter.

The post war years were bleak. The number of deaths suffered by families, communities and friends in the Great War was enormous. At the end of four devastating years, the newspaper headlines reported strikes, economic depression and adversity.

Local unemployment and hardship was recorded through the long list of applications for help to the Newbury Board of Guardians.

The end of the war meant that Lord Carnarvon could return to archaeology and Egypt. As previously mentioned, Carnarvon had finally acquired the long sought concession for the Valley of the Kings in 1914, but only now could he begin to plan his explorations with Carter.

In March 1919, Lady Carnarvon and their daughter, Lady Evelyn, arrived in Egypt. This was no easy journey so soon after the War. Many ships had been used as troopships and were unsanitary and there remained a few floating mines in the Mediterranean Sea, which sank other boats in 1919.

Above. Bretby Hall, Derbyshire, which Lord Carnarvon sold in 1915 to raise finance for his continuing explorations in Egypt.

There was general unrest in Egypt at th[e] time and so Lady Carnarvon and Lad[y] Evelyn returned to England for the[ir] safety. Lord Carnarvon stayed on i[n] Cairo.

Sir William Garstin

General Sir John Maxwell

Carnarvon had a deep interest in Egyptian politics, had a great liking for many Egyptians and had their confidence. Sir William Garstin, Director of Antiquities and General Sir John Maxwell, Military Commander i[n] Egypt, bot[h] acknowledge[d] that Carnarvo[n] was a we[ll] respecte[d] expert o[n] politics, ente[r]tainin[g] Egyptian dele[gations a[t] Highclere an[d] in London.

Lord Carnarvon had now recovered fro[m] appendicitis, but Howard Carter was no[t] at all well. It was his turn to undergo a[n] abdominal operation, this time for th[e] removal of his gall bladder by Sir Berkele[y] Moynihan in Lady Carnarvon's nursin[g] home. He recuperated in Seamore Plac[e] the Carnarvon's London home.

Almina's father, Alfred de Rothschil[d] had died in 1918, leaving a large part of h[is] fortune including his beautiful hous[e]

...eamore Place) and art collection to his daughter, Almina. During this time, Carter helped Carnarvon organise the catalogue for an exhibition at the Burlington Fine Arts Club. Carnarvon and Carter then left for Egypt on January 18th, 1922.

On February 5th, Lord Carnarvon arrived in Luxor. He stayed until March 29th before returning home. Carter had rested part of the time in Cairo and had spent other time making purchases with Lord Carnarvon.

Lord Carnarvon spent a lot of time with different ministers; conditions were difficult in Egypt, as nationalist sentiments surfaced which led to riots and confrontation.

Carnarvon's circumstances were increasingly straightened. He had sold his Nottinghamshire house and estate, and he was now selling land in Somerset.

After the spring of 1922, Carnarvon was feeling increasingly under financial pressure at home, selling land between Highclere and Newbury, trying to pay post war taxes, selling horses and finding no artefacts or archaeological leads in the Valley of the Kings.

In June 1922, Howard Carter was staying with Lord Carnarvon and they went racing with the rest of the house party to Newbury.

Carnarvon still had the concession and Carter, in a moment of recklessness, said he would pay the excavation costs for another season.

Carnarvon both respected and was fond of Carter, so he offered his support for one last year in the Valley. There was one area they wanted to explore, which was normally the main part of the tourist route by the tomb of Ramesses VI.

Carter decided he would like to go early, before Carnarvon normally travelled, and before most of the tourists descended on the Valley, in order to explore this particular area.

Above. Lord Carnarvon's actual letters to his land agent, Major Rutherford, written on the day of Carnarvon's arrival in Egypt, 5th February 1922.

4

Materials and Workmanship

ord Carnarvon and Howard Carter achieved worldwide fame for the discovery of one particular tomb in 1922. During the previous sixteen years, however, Lord Carnarvon had acquired through excavation and purchase, an extraordinary collection of Egyptian Antiquities.

He had collected about 1,400 separate items. He also donated various works of art to the British Museum, the Newbury Museum and lent other pieces to London exhibitions.

The majority of his Collection was later sold to the Metropolitan Museum of New York by his widow to pay Death Duties. It was catalogued for his widow by Howard Carter who had left a "few unimportant items" at Highclere.

They were wholly forgotten about until they were rediscovered upon the death of the 6th Earl of Carnarvon, some 63 years later.

They now form the basis of the Collection seen by visitors to Highclere Castle today.

The Antiquities Collection is organised thematically, and this chapter follows the route an Exhibition visitor takes. Although ancient Egyptian civilisation ended over 2,000 years ago, we have a wealth of knowledge about the Egyptians' customs, religion, writing and culture because they quarried and used stone: granite, limestone or sandstone, to record and celebrate their civilisation.

Some spectacular engineering works involved moving massive blocks of stone some distance along the Nile. Other work was much more intricate and used tools of dolorite and bronze, tipped with flint and copper.

Granite and quartzite were also extracted and used for some monumental statues and, because they were so hard, visitors can still admire these statues today.

Gold and silver (which was very rare) were used mainly for decoration in Royal tombs or for coins. The soil and clay from the river Nile provided clay for pottery for everyday vessels.

Calcite is the mineral name for alabaster. Egyptian calcite has been extensively worked for centuries near Suez and Asyut. There are also many ancient quarries in the hills overlooking the plain of Tell el-Amarna.

Lord Carnarvon and Howard Carter discovered 13 calcite jars in 1920 in the debris at the entrance to the tomb of the Pharaoh Merneptah (1212-1202BC) in the Valley of the Kings. Lady Carnarvon, who accompanied her husband on this dig, was so excited, she helped dig them out.

The cartouche on the jar shown here is that of Ramesses II, Merneptah's father. Others bore inscriptions suggesting they came from Merneptah's burial. Objects from the mummification were buried near the tomb. The jars had been used to contain oils for the embalming and wrapping of the mummy of Merneptah.

Merneptah's father, Ramesses the Great (II) was one of the most famous of all Egyptian Pharaohs, creating the temple at Abu Simbel, the great fallen statues at Karnak, chiseling his name deeply into monuments and temples so it could never easily be erased and, reputedly, fathering 200 children.

He had created a greater Egypt and brought back prizes from many lands, including cedars from Lebanon. He had outlived many of his sons and was succeeded by his thirteenth son Merneptah. His mummy was found and it showed he died at an advanced age. Merneptah was Pharaoh for ten years and was succeeded by Seti II.

The calcite jar found in 1920, showing the cartouche of Ramesses II

Stone Vessels

A wide range of stone could be quarried in Egypt with special care being taken to choose beautiful examples for funerary vessels.

Vessels and bowls were often made from *schist*, a type of siltstone from the Eastern Desert, which lies between the Nile and the Red Sea.

This schist dish is 5,000 years old and was probably part of the funerary equipment of a nobleman. It was thought he would

A rushwork model sieve and collection of wooden and bronze instruments and tools (1390-1353BC), including three small flint blades and two small arrowheads

The 5,000 year old 'schist' dish

use it to eat from in the Afterlife.

These hard stone bowls were replaced with calcite and model vessels over the next 1,000 years, which were easier to make.

Flask, dish and jar, c.1540BC

Pottery

Pottery tended to be for everyday use. It was often made of clay from the River Nile.

The taller jars and bottles date from 1390-1353BC, time of the Pharaoh Akhenaten. Tall vases were popular, and they were buried in the tombs containing provisions for the next world.

The pottery flask, pottery dish and pottery jar date from the time of the Pharaoh Kamose (1554-1549BC), 17th Dynasty. He unified Egypt at the beginning of the 18th Dynasty.

They were all found under Queen Hatshepsut's Valley Temple in Tomb 37, by Lord Carnarvon and Howard Carter.

Tall pottery bottles found under Queen Hatshepsut's Temple, c.1350BC

Wooden instruments

Instruments are made from copper or bronze for carving and making objects. Egyptian artisans produced fine joinery, constructing wooden boxes, coffins, stools, and beautiful model boats.

Tools and model tools would be buried in tombs, so they were ready for the next world. The oldest bronze tools date to the 4th Dynasty: chisels, one complete and one broken; an adze blade, a hatchet and some rasps; three small flint blades and two small arrowheads.

Metals such as lead or iron were highly prized due to their scarcity, and either the metals or the finished goods were imported into Egypt.

Two blue bowls made from faience, the earliest known artificial ceramic

Faience

Faience is a glazed ceramic material, composed of crushed quartz or sand. Egypt, being rich in sand, provided unlimited quantities for the manufacture of faience. Quartz was ground down and fused with malachite and blue azurite to create the blue colour. A weak solution of salt or natron (a naturally occurring form of soda ash, much used by the ancient Egyptians) would bind it together.

It was used for bowls, jewellery, rings and wadjet-eye, amulets, pectorals and shabti figures. Faience glistens with light and was thought to symbolise re-birth.

Two blue faience bowls were found by the 5th Earl in tomb 24 (under Queen Hatshepsut's Temple) in 1910. They are decorated with Lotus flowers, and one is inscribed with an invocation to the goddess, Hathor.

The Lotus flower closes at night to re-emerge and bloom the next day, so it became a symbol for re-birth. It represented Upper Egypt, whilst papyrus represented Lower Egypt. The motifs were painted in black before firing.

The tomb of Teta-Ky, a King's son, who became Mayor of Thebes.

Offering Table of Teta-Ky

In 1908, Lord Carnarvon returned to Egypt for his second season of excavation. He had been given a concession to dig at Dra' abu el-Naga' on the west bank of the Nile opposite the modern city of Luxor, known in ancient times as Thebes.

After two week's hard digging, Lord Carnarvon discovered an important 18th Dynasty tomb, which proved to be that of a King's son: Teta-Ky.

In the tomb, a fragment of a statue describes Teta-Ky as 'Mayor of the Southern City' i.e. Thebes. This is the earliest reference to the office of a Mayor.

The tomb contained an offering tab displayed on the page opposite.

These tables are thought to rece offerings such as oil or water. The wat could run along the grooves, perhaps metaphor for the rivers the deceas might travel.

Photograph of tomb above, tomb walls left and Offering Table opposite by the 5th Earl, 1909.

28

Adornment

Make u

A diorette palette, pestle, tweeze
and kohl pots and sticks from th
12th Dynasty (c.1963-1650B

A collection of silver bracelets
(c.304-30BC) found by Lord
Carnarvon at Tell el- Balamun
in 1911

The Egyptians were concerned with personal grooming in this life and the next. Containers for kohl for enhancing the eyes were very common. Part of the custom prescribed in the 'Book of the Dead', states that the deceased must be painted with black eye paint, so this would need to be included in the burial.

Portraits of ancient Egyptians consistently show meticulously outlined and ornamented eyes. It is virtually impossible to find a portrait of an ancient Egyptian whose eyes are not decorated.

Eye make up provided spiritual prote tion as well. The Egyptian word for ey palette seems to derive from their wo for 'protect'. An unadorned and, thu unprotected eye was believed vulnerab to the 'Evil Eye'.

Outlining the eyes, therefore, became personal protective amulet drawn rig upon the skin; an amulet that once a plied could not be lost or misplaced.

Jewellery

…any magnificent pieces were found in …ypt. Necklaces and rings were also …ed as amulets, to protect the wearer or …testify to their deference to the gods.

…ver was imported from Asia by way of …bute or trade. Silver was a more

highly prized material than gold. Jewellery such as bracelets, however, were often

…e first target for grave-robbers and …ly rare examples remain today.

…ue faience ball beads may well be …sociated with the scarab beetle which …ys its eggs inside a ball of dung. The …arabs became a symbol for re-birth and …surrection and the beetle was wor-…ipped as the god Khepra. He was

…ought to push the sun across the sky …d then roll it through the Underworld. …carabs were often popular as amulets. …e heart scarabs were to protect the …ost important part of the body in …gyptian religion.

Beaded flail of faience and carnelian beads (1540-1075BC), found by Lord Carnarvon and Howard Carter in Tomb 70 at Deir el Bahri.

Symbols

The flail was originally an agricultural tool used for threshing, but it also became the symbol for the God Osiris, symbolising the Pharaoh's role as provider of food for his people. The decorative flail here dates from the time of the Pharaoh Ahmose, c.1550BC.

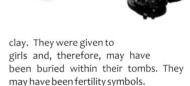

The paddle doll was originally painted and had long beaded hair. It is nearly 4,000 years old and had a face made of

clay. They were given to girls and, therefore, may have been buried within their tombs. They may have been fertility symbols.

Trinket Boxes

These were found with mummy beads in Tomb 25 (under Queen Hatshepsut's Valley Temple) by the 5th Earl and are possibly 4,000 years old.

They usually, as here, contained mummy beads which, like amulets, protected the dead person.

18th Dynasty Faience Jewellery

Above right. Faience mummy attachment in the shape of a kneeling figure of Isis, (c.304-30BC), her wings outstretched with holes around the edge for the attachment.

Left. Faience bead necklace.

Right. Fragment from a faience pectoral (c.1390-1353BC), 18th Dynasty.

Archer's Wrist Guard

This is designed to protect the inner arm as the bow string was released. It is a rare and unusual piece, elaborately decorated with a series of bound captives symbolising the traditional enemies of Egypt: the Nubians from the South and the Syrians from the Mediterranean coasts.

It may well have been discovered near the tomb of Amenophis III.

The Egyptian archers used to stand on the back of light chariots. They were organised into well trained units able quickly to out-flank an enemy army with devastating effect, and were able to fire their light arrows for up to 400yds.

Musical instruments

Music played an important part in Egyptian life and many scenes are illustrated in temples and tombs.

The earliest instruments in Egypt were boomerang-shaped clappers, which were known, not only in Egypt, but also from southern Palestine as early as the 5th millennium BC.

During the Pharaonic period, they were often decorated with hands, as here. They were also used rather like castanets.

The sistrum was a sacred, musical instrument, often made from wood or metal so the faience handle here is quite unusual. Above the handle there would have been a frame in the shape of an ankh (a religious symbol) and small metal disks strung within the frame, which rattled when the instrument was shaken by hand.

The head of Hathor was often depicted on the handle. The Egyptian name was sesheshet which probably derives from the sounds the instrument makes: a soft jangling sound, resembling a breeze blowing through papyrus reeds.

Green glazed faience sistrum handle (c.1540-1075BC) found at Deir el Bahri

Ivory clappers (c.1987-1640BC) which are shaped into hands and pierced so they can be held like a castanet. A pale green faience bell decorated with the god Bes.

33

Writing and Seals

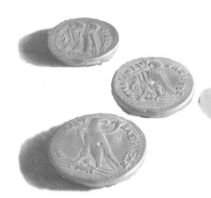

The ancient Egyptian language is known from texts spanning nearly 4,000 years. The development of the language is grouped into three periods: Old Egyptian, Middle Egyptian and Late Egyptian. The time span means that it would be as difficult for early Egyptians to understand late Egyptian language as Anglo Saxon 'English' would be for us in England today.

Hieroglyphs were abandoned in the 4th century AD, as they were associated with a superceded Royal family and pagan gods. The unity of script and art was used to describe the Pharonic religious beliefs. They were used in temples and tombs carved in stone.

A very small minority could read and write hieroglyphs. Later, hieratic and then demotic script were used to record, write and calculate. The writing was usually done on wooden boards, sometimes linen if it was a funerary text, and usually in black using a carbon pigment.

Reed quills were used to write. Papyrus, the most common surface used, has rarely survived, as it is fragile and vulnerable to water damage. Thus, a greater proportion of the history which has survived was written in hieroglyphs.

For the next 1,700 years until the present day, however, hieroglyphs were ignored and considered obscure symbols from a pagan civilisation.

Ancient Egyptian Hieroglyphs

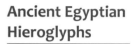

Hieroglyph is used both as a term for a language and for the individual characters that comprise it.

Hieroglyph is actually a Greek word meaning sacred carving, because the Greeks observed that the Egyptian writings were mostly on the walls of temples and funerary reliefs an figures.

In many ways, hieroglyphs are a form c art: beautiful to look at, sometime coloured, communicating both sound and informa- tion. There is a unique unity of character and image: it is not just a text. There are far more subtle

interactions of symbolism and personif cation that are lost in translation.

The hieroglyphic signs interwove pic tures, words and thoughts. The languag consisted of over 2,000 character whereas the English alphabet consist only of 26. Each hieroglyphic characte takes the form of a common object fron their day.

The direction of writing in the hieroglyphic script varied. It could be vertical from top to bottom or from right to left, or left to right in horizontal lines.

The earliest known examples of hieroglyphs in Egypt have been dated to 3,400BC. It may be the earliest form of writing in the world.

We have no idea, however, where Egyptian hieroglyphs came from. They do not seem to have evolved over a period of centuries, but appeared almost suddenly.

What is strange is that hieroglyphs seemed to appear out of nowhere, fully formed as a script and, presumably, as a language. It would also seem that the earliest use was in the Nile Delta region of Egypt or, perhaps, it may have been brought into Egypt from outside.

The Egyptians believed that language was a divine gift and plays on words linked the earthly world with that of the gods. Names were more than words: they were representations of the being or person.

Thus, the destruction of a name, often practiced by Pharaohs of their predecessors, was more than removing the name; it was destroying the actual being and presence.

Opposite. Ptolemaic coins cast in bronze, found in Upper Egypt, (c.300BC). Cartouches carved in ivory, often inlaid into furniture.
Above, Hieroglyphics carved into a sandstone wall. Photograph by the 8th Earl, 2006.

The Rosetta Stone

The discovery of the 'Rosetta Stone' in Egypt in 1799 was the first step on the road to the understanding of hieroglyphs. The inscriptions on the stone are written in three different scripts: Egyptian hieroglyphs, Demotic (another Egyptian language derived from the hieroglyphic script), and Greek.

It is a slab of black basalt stone discovered by Napoleon's soldiers near the seaside town of Rosetta in lower Egypt. On Napoleon's defeat, the stone became the property of George III, who gave it to the British Museum in London. It dates from 196BC, and is inscribed by the ancient Egyptians with a Royal decree praising their King, Ptolemy V.

Thomas Young

Copies were made of the scripts on the stone and European scholars tried to solve the mystery of the ancient Egyptian text. They began work on the Demotic text, since it seemed to be like an alphabetic cursive script.

The English physicist Thomas Young made a breakthrough when he realised that the cartouches represented important names and, since some of them were

The hieroglyph for Ramesses

foreign names, (Ptolemis or Ramesses), he deduced they had to be spelt phonetically.

He matched the letters of Ptolemy with the hieroglyphs, and correlated the hieroglyphs with their correct phonetic values. He took his work no further

The hieroglyph for Ptolemis

believing the other Egyptian signs were only pictograms.

Jean-François Champollion

The French linguist, Jean-François Champollion, had also been working on the texts. He was fluent in Coptic and was able to take Young's work further. In 1822, he gave a famous lecture in Paris showing that hieroglyphs were a writing system and consisted of semantic signs, phonetic signs and pictograms.

Over the next few years, he was able to identify phonetic signs for most of the hieroglyphs and began to lay out a grammar for ancient Egyptian as well.

Throughout the time of the ancient Egyptian civilisation, the hieroglyphs and paintings in the tombs were the key connections to the next world. They were crucial to the preservation of the Afterlife. Today, they are also the key to our understanding of ancient Egyptian beliefs.

Ancient Egyptian Hieratic Script

The Hieratic script was probably developed more or less at the same time as the Hieroglyphic script. It was used throughout Egypt for day to day purposes such as keeping records and accounts and writing letters.

This script was used until the 26th Dynasty. By that time, however, it was only used for religious texts, while the Demotic script was used for most other purposes. Hieratic script continued to be used by the priestly class for several more centuries, at least into the third century AD.

Hieratic script was first written vertically but, from about 2,000BC, was always written from right to left. It was developed to speed up the writing process and was used for everyday memoranda or contracts. Since it was often written on papyrus, there are few records which have actually survived several thousand years.

It is difficult now to estimate the extent of Egyptian literary culture. The range of incomplete fragments testifies to the possible breadth of astronomical records, astrological charts, hymns, poems, medical prescriptions, contracts, arithmetical calculations, instructions for religious rites, dream interpretations and maxims for life.

Phonetic examples

Hieroglyphic	Hieratic	English
		h
		m
		f

Hieratic script was the first writing system taught to students. Only a small minority could read and write in Egypt and such an ability would lead to state service and income, as opposed to hard manual labour.

Determinative examples

Hieroglyphic	Hieratic	English
		writing
		man
		foreign country

Papyrus was the most usual writing surface, but leather and plaster on wood were also quite common. Pens were made from reeds and were used on dampened pigment, held over the writing surface like a water colour brush.

Hieratic alphabet had both character glyphs, which were phonetic and characters, which were determinatives, which embodied a whole idea or gave added meaning and direction.

Ancient Egyptian Demotic Script

The word Demotic derives from the Greek word for commoner; thus it was the popular script, the one used in everyday life.

Demotic script was a development of Hieratic script. It is the second script inscribed on the Rosetta Stone. It has a cursive form: the signs are flowing and joined. French and British academics assumed that it was based on an alphabet and had phonetic values. Therefore, they tried to decipher the Demotic script using the Greek to locate proper names in the text.

Sylvestre de Sacy

A French orientalist, Sylvestre de Sacy, started working on the Demotic script in 1802. He began to identify the proper names and try to find the corresponding names in the Demotic text. His work was extended by one of his students, a Swedish diplomat called Johan Akerblad.

Akerblad identified the Demotic proper names such as Bernice, Arsinoe, and Ptolos and built up a Demotic alphabet of 29 letters. Half of them were actually correct. Then, he demonstrated that the phonetic signs used to write the names were also used to spell ordinary words such as 'Egyptian,' 'Greek,' 'temple,' 'love'. Some of the script is, however, symbolic and not phonetic, and it was not until 1850 that the German scholar Heinrich Karl Brugsch made the final breakthrough. After years of research, he published a complete translation of the Demotic writing.

Demotic script was partly derived from simplified hieroglyphic signs. It was used for business and legal documents, private letters, religious, scientific, and medical and magical texts, mummy tags, funerary and administrative stelae and to complain about various matters. There were, however, many variations of sign so that words had to be learnt as a unit rather than learning individual letters or combinations. Demotic papyri, especially business contracts, survive in greater numbers because they are not as ancient. Demotic script was written on papyrus and also engraved on stone or on wood.

The script was used for more than a thousand years. It was first used during the 26th Dynasty (the Ptolemaic period around 650BC), through the Greek period, to the time of Roman rule in Egypt, when it more or less disappeared.

Carnarvon Papyrus I

During the 4th century AD, Demotic writing was gradually replaced by the Greek-derived Coptic alphabet. It may well have been much closer to the spoken language than the more elaborate classical hieroglyphs.

In 1911, while working among the Ptolemaic vaulted tombs above Queen Hatshepsut's Temple, Lord Carnarvon and Howard Carter discovered two Demotic papyri, Carnarvon Papyri I and II, which they dated from the time of Ptolemy, 205-180BC. These Papyri are Sale Agreements for temple land between different contractors.

One Papyrus is reproduced here from the original photographs of the Papyri which are contained in the book "Five Year's Explorations at Thebes, A Record of Work Done 1907-1911", published by the 5th Earl of Carnarvon in 1912.

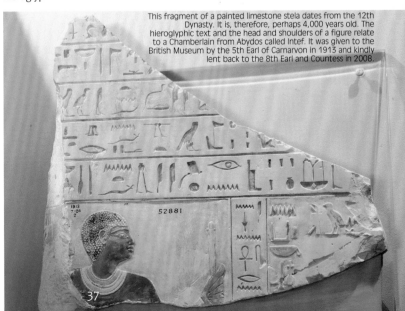

This fragment of a painted limestone stela dates from the 12th Dynasty. It is, therefore, perhaps 4,000 years old. The hieroglyphic text and the head and shoulders of a figure relate to a Chamberlain from Abydos called Intef. It was given to the British Museum by the 5th Earl of Carnarvon in 1913 and kindly lent back to the 8th Earl and Countess in 2008.

The Book of the Dead

This is the common name for ancient Egyptian funerary texts known as The Book of Coming (or Going) Forth By Day.

Karl Richard Lepsius

The name 'Book of the Dead' was the invention of the German Egyptologist Karl Richard Lepsius, who published a selection of some texts in 1842.

The 'Book of the Dead' is a collection of spells, charms, passwords, numbers and magical formulae for use by the deceased in the Afterlife. This described many of the basic tenets of Egyptian mythology.

They were intended to guide the dead through the various trials that they would encounter, before reaching the Underworld. They do not, however, prescribe moral codes or revelations about the current world. They were concerned with the Afterlife.

However, without a successful moral existence in this world, no person could hope for the Afterlife. Knowledge of the appropriate spells was considered essential to achieving happiness after death.

The spells or prayers were later written on papyrus now known as scrolls

A papyrus fragment from the 'Book of the Dead' (c.1190-1075BC), 20th Dynasty and depicts a woman admiring the god Osiris

and buried inside the sarcophagus with the deceased, presumably so that it would be both portable and close at hand.

The 'Going Forth by Day' represents a strong image of the soul emerging into the sunlight again. The sun god Re was a major figure at this point. Many of the Pharaohs' names were compounded with the word 'Re', and some o f t h gods were also given the addition epithet 'Re'.

The more local gods such as Sob Re, Khnum Re, Min-Re were given national status by combining them with the word Re. The deceased wished to enter Re's entourage and join him in one of his celestial boats.

Fragment of a wall decoration from the tomb of Bakenrenef, (664-610BC painted on limestone. Bakenrenef was the Vizier (Prime Minister) of Egypt under King Psamtek I (26th Dynasty). He was buried at a tomb at Saqqara.

The hieroglyphs form part of spell 22 from the Book of the Dead. The text here refers to the dead man being given back his mouth, so he may speak to Osiris, the

Wood panel fragment, showing the remains of two columns of hieroglyphic text.

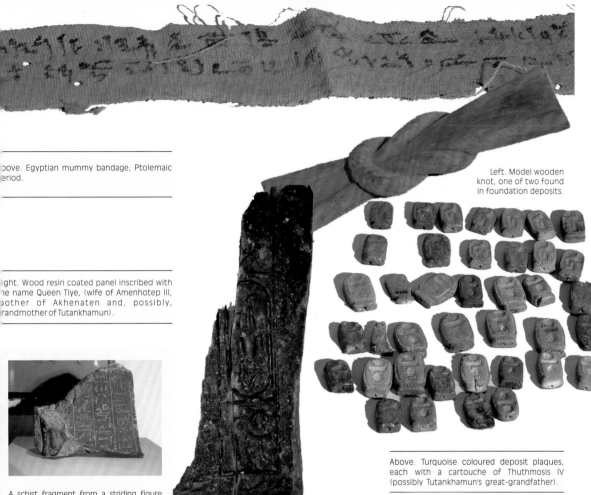

Above. Egyptian mummy bandage, Ptolemaic period.

Right. Wood resin coated panel inscribed with the name Queen Tiye, (wife of Amenhotep III, mother of Akhenaten and, possibly, grandmother of Tutankhamun).

Left. Model wooden knot, one of two found in foundation deposits.

A schist fragment from a striding figure from Tell el-Balamun 700BC.

Tell el-Balamun lies 20 km south of the Mediterranean and 5km west of a branch of the Nile. The mud mounds and plains contain the remains of a temple, town and necropolis, probably from the Ptolemaic period and later.

Lord Carnarvon and Howard Carter applied for the concession in 1912. They found some small objects including some shabti scarabs, amulets, jewellery and pottery.

One of the most important pieces discovered is this fragment from a funerary statuette. The unique importance is that it invokes Amun-Re Lord of Sambehedet and Osiris of the Porch of Behdet of Lower Egypt.

The owner of the Statue was probably a priest of Amun at Sambehedet and helps strengthen the case for this city "The Northern Porch" being here at Tell el-Balamun.

Above. Turquoise coloured deposit plaques, each with a cartouche of Thuthmosis IV (possibly Tutankhamun's great-grandfather).

Above. Fragments of faience vessels inscribed with the name of Amenophis III.

Above. The cartouche of Queen Tiye, as inscribed on the wood resin panel, above centre.

Faces & Figures

Statue of Akhenate
father of Tutankhamu
(Cairo Museun

Egyptian religion was polytheistic, which creates a gulf between today's religions and the Egyptian civilisation.

Our own religious beliefs immediately suggest that their religion was inferior and primitive. Different gods bore differing values which seemed, at first, to oppose each other. It can seem quite bewildering.

However, there was a major religious shift during the reign of Akhenaten. He proclaimed the cult of the 'one god', the 'Aten', of which he was the divine embodiment. Yet, it would be wrong to say that Akhenaten's monotheism was a more superior religious approach.

The Egyptian gods, such as Amun or Osiris, often embodied conflicting characteristics. Individuals could choose the gods through whom they wanted to define their life; there was no single message.

Different towns or areas preferred one god over another, so a traveller might invoke a local god in the place where he was staying, as well as his own home town god to ask for his protection and blessing.

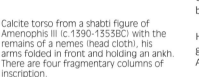

Calcite torso from a shabti figure of Amenophis III (c.1390-1353BC) with the remains of a nemes (head cloth), his arms folded in front and holding an ankh. There are four fragmentary columns of inscription.

Egyptian deities were not merely named they were illustrated and the word 'face is often used in the epithets applied t the gods. It is thought to have a muc broader meaning than our English wor It also incorporates the vision, sigh head and aspect.

If a god manifests itself as an animal, suc as a jackal or a cow, it does not take c the characteristics of that animal. It simply an emblem, a temporary home.

A statue of an Apis bull (c.716BC)

Shabti

[th]e Egyptians introduced shabtis into [th]eir tombs to undertake manual labour [in] the Afterlife, such as to till the soil.

shabtis were especially treasured, as faience was symbolic of death and rebirth.

Below is shown the lower part from a calcite shabti figure with the cartouche of Queen Tiye, the Great Royal Wife of Amenophis III.

She regularly appears beside Amenophis III in stelae, statues, tomb and temple reliefs.

This was, perhaps, the first time that an Egyptian Royal wife was ever given equal precedence with the Pharaoh.

[Th]e word probably derives from the [E]gyptian word to answer. They would [m]agically appear in the next world. They [w]ere first introduced into tombs in the [18]th Dynasty.

[Sh]abtis were also made to resemble the [d]eceased and were beautifully carved [w]orks of art in their own right, such as the [ca]lcite head of Amenophis III, shown [ab]ove.

[R]oyal Shabtis were first found at the very [b]eginning of the 18th Dynasty. [Tu]tankhamun had 413 shabtis, Seti perhaps 700 faience shabtis. Faience

The lower part from a calcite shabti figure with the cartouche of Queen Tiye, the Great Royal Wife of Amenophis III.

Animals and deities

Animals were as important as the landscape, rivers and plants in making up the Egyptian world. They were domesticated and hunted, admired and utilised. Many animals acquired religious significance.

Some animal characteristics became attributes of the gods, thus the jackal was associated with Anubis, the falcon with Horus, the cow with Hathor. Some animals were held to be sacred and some animals were mummified, perhaps because they were much loved pets or animals symbolically representing an image in a temple.

One of the most important animal cults was that of the bull, which appeared in Egyptian writings as far back as the 1st Dynasty. The ancients believed that the powerful bull represented the personality of the king, his strength and courage. The bull was considered sacred and an incarnation of the God Osiris.

Lord Carnarvon and Howard Carter found the bronze figure, shown above, of an Apis Bull at Tell el-Balamun. It has a sun disk between its horns.

A bronze statue of an Ibis

Horus is one of the most ancient Deities of Ancient Egypt. He is represented as a falcon and his name is believed to mean above or, the far off.

The little stearite figure of Isis and Horus illustrates that Isis was a vital link between the gods and mankind.

She was a very powerful goddess who cared about her people. The pharaoh was her son, the living Horus.

Isis & Horus

The sphinx designates a type of statue joining a human head to the body of a lion. It symbolises sovereignty, combining the strength of the lion with human

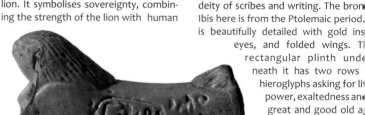

Sphinx

The Ibis was sacred to the birth of the g Thoth, the god of the moon and patr deity of scribes and writing. The bron Ibis here is from the Ptolemaic period. is beautifully detailed with gold ins eyes, and folded wings. T rectangular plinth und neath it has two rows hieroglyphs asking for li power, exaltedness an great and good old a for Horwedja.

The bronze figure of the God Hapocrates was found at Tell el-Balamun. It is another figure to represent Horus.

Bronze statue of the child god Hapocrates (c.716BC)

intelligence. The statue can be dated to the late 25th Dynasty, as there are cartouches of King Shabka on each side.

Sekhmet is depicted as a lion headed woman. She was a fearsome Deity and could be both a creative and a destructive force. The name Sekhmet is derived from the Egyptian word Sekhem, meaning power or might. She is portrayed here as a glazed amuletic figure seated on a throne, holding a sistrum. See also page 80 for the golden statue of Sekhmet found in the Treasury of the tomb of Tutankhamun.

Sekhmet

Hea

The Egyptia associated t frog with fertil and resurrecti and so Heq the fro goddess, w associated wi childbirth.

Bes was an ancient Egyptian dwarf god, who was a god of protection against evil with his tambourine or harp, swords and maces. He also became a god of childbirth, frightening away all of the evil spirits that could kill babies or newborn children.

Later, he was given a wife, known as Beset, a female version of the dwarf god, who presided over protection, pleasure and childbirth.

set

ranite statue of Amun-
e and his consort Mut

uring the New Kingdom, (18th Dynasty), nun was regarded as the principal god, e father of the gods. He combined thin himself the two contrasting facets divinity: the hidden, (the essential sence that cannot be seen), and the vealed. The Pharaoh derived his power om Amun-Re and, in return, dedicated mples to him.

ut, his wife, was considered the divine other from which the cosmos emerged.

nun-Re's and Mut's features are those of tankhamun and his wife Ankhesenamun d, therefore, date from c 1325BC.

his statue has been kindly lent to the h Earl and Countess of Carnarvon by e British Museum).

The Antiquities Collection

The story of Irtyru

Coffins and mummification

Lord Carnarvon and Howard Carter discovered this coffin belonging to a lady, Irtyru, in tomb No 5 at the Eastern end of a path leading to Deir el-Bahri in Thebes. It was found with two other painted coffins belonging to her husband, Pad de Khonsu, and their son, Pademun.

Lord Carnarvon wrote of the thrill of discovery and of the feeling that he was touching such an old part of history and ritual.

The bouquets of cornflowers and wreaths by the coffins were still there from when the last person entered the tomb 3,500 years ago. The decoration and care given to the internment indicate that these three people had been well off and from a noble family.

THE COFFIN UNTOUCHED SINCE THE DAY IT WAS PLACED THERE

The coffin is made from cedar covered with a coarse linen and painted. Irtyru was wrapped in a dark terracotta linen

shroud. Lying at her head was a diadem of leaves and petals sewn together. She was probably 35 years old at the time of her death.

Also displayed are a discarded garment, a galabaya and linen bandages in which the embalmed body was wrapped.

Linen was used for many household purposes and woven in large quantities. The strips of linen used here would probably have been torn from sheets or garments which is why there are fringes or stripes.

The ancient Egyptians believed that the heart recorded all of the good and bad deeds of a person's life. They considered the heart to be the centre of thought, memory and emotion. It was thought to be the most important organ in the body.

Above: the actual bandages and bones found in Irtyru's tomb, together with some small shabtis as found by Lord Carnarvon and Howard Carter in Deir el-Bahri, 1908.

ove. The "Ceremony of the Heart"
inted on Irtyru's coffin, on display in the
tiquities Collection.

People would be judged after death in accordance with their deeds in this life, so many a noble person proclaimed their charitable acts on behalf of the weak or poor. There were constant threats even to pure and good souls, so it was not an easy journey into the Afterlife.

To the right of the scales, Nut waits to accompany the deceased to the Afterlife and on the left are six of the most important gods; Osiris, Isis, Nepthys, Sekhmet and Sobek who stand in judgment of the ceremony.

The decoration on the lid of the coffin shows the outstretched wings of Isis, protecting the soul or spirit of the deceased and the solar disc, often depicted by the scarab beetle, as the symbol of rebirth.

he heart was essential for re-birth in the terlife and, unlike other internal or- ns, it was never removed and em- lmed separately, because its presence the body was crucial.

he ancient Egyptians believed that the ead person would face certain trials on e journey to the Afterlife, to discover hether he or she was worthy of the ext life.

the base of the coffin of Itryru is a inting of Nut (pronounced noot), the ddess of the sky and the heavens. Her ms are extended around the sides of e coffin to protect Irtyru on her journey the Afterlife.

each hand, she holds an 'ankh', the mbol of life. Nut's name still resonates day through the French word for night, nuit'.

In the 'Ceremony of the Heart', the deceased person's heart is weighed against the 'feather of truth'. The image symbolically represents the moral worth of the dead person. The heart must balance, or weigh less than, the feather for the deceased to enter the Afterlife. The beast, Ammut, ('devourer of the heart') which was a combination of a lion, a crocodile and a hippopotamus, waits below the scales ready to devour the heart should it weigh more than the feather.

Ma'at, the goddess of truth, stands symbolically below the scales. The baboon sitting above represents Thoth, the god of writing, or the scribe who records the event. The fear of the final judgment is highlighted throughout the 'Book of the Dead' and the stelae and paintings in tombs throughout Egyptian history.

The hieroglyphics on the coffin record good character and helpful detail, such as the provisions of beer and bread, oxen, fowl, incense and clothing for the god Osiris from Irtyru, the deceased.

Above. The painting of the goddess 'Nut' on the base of Irtyru's coffin, on display in the Antiquities Collection.

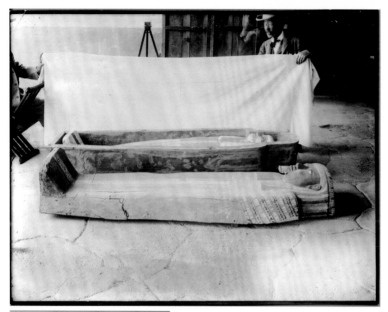

Lord Carnarvon and Howard Carter in Deir el-Bahri, 1908. The coffin of the husband of Irtyru, Pademun.

Mummification

One of the best known rituals, practiced by the Egyptians, was mummification. Irtyru's body was mummified and first placed in the coffin and then in the tomb, all of which helped ensure she could complete her journey to the next world and her resurrection.

Just as undertakers bury the dead today, so skilled Egyptian artisans passed down the traditions and knowledge so that the whole ritual of grieving and burial carried on in much the same manner for nearly three thousand years.

The embalmers were respected and accorded similar privileges to priests. The hieroglyph for natron, (a naturally-occurring form of soda ash), is combined with a banner to signify its divine nature and it was carefully stored in a pouch.

The deceased first remained at home for up to 4 days to allow for a period of mourning. The embalming process took 42 days. That was then followed by 30 days of rituals. However, poorer families could only pay for simple burials, either straight into the sand of the desert (the cheapest option) or with a basic embalming process (a middle route).

Irtyru's family could afford the best option. Her body would have been taken to an embalmers' workshop in a coffin, removed and laid on a table. Her family would have taken away the coffin.

The embalmers would first extract the brain by threading an iron hook through her nose. Nothing was done with the brain, as its purpose was perhaps little understood by the Egyptians.

Then, her side would have been slit with sharp Ethiopian stone. The cavities a next washed out with herbs and pal wine. The heart was always carefully le in the body but the other organs we removed and preserved.

Wealthy clients could afford beautiful decorated Canopic jars, in which t preserve the organs. The body wa covered with natron, natural soda as which was found throughout Egypt. desiccated the body tissues and wa thought to purify the deceased. It wa left for at least 40 days.

At the end of this period, the body wa washed and different herbs, such a myrr or frankincense, were used to anoint th body. It was wrapped in strips of line usually torn from tablecloths.

The family then returned with the coffi and the wrapped figure was place inside and taken to the tomb.

Irtyru's coffin and tomb were typical of many discovered by Lord Carnarvon and Howard Carter.

The coffin and works of art in the Antiquities Collection at Highclere Castle represent only a fraction of Lord Carnarvon's original collection.

The records and achievements earned both men the respect of their contemporaries and have since provided a lasting legacy for Egyptologists.

The sixteen years of collaboration between the two men has been, in the most part, ignored. This collaboration was over-shadowed by the discovery, at the end of 1922, of the Tomb of Tutankhamun during the last season the two Englishmen worked together.

The map below shows that Carter had, over the period from 1917 to 1921, divided the Valley of the Kings into a series of grids. No significant discoveries were made during these years in any of the grid sections worked on.

In June 1922, Howard Carter was staying at Highclere Castle for a race meeting at Newbury, the local course. Lord Carnarvon explained to Howard Carter that he could no longer continue with his excavation work in Egypt, as he was struggling financially.

In a moment of recklessness, Carter offered to finance this work himself. Carnarvon, however, was persuaded by his good friend's kind offer to pay for one last expedition. It was then agreed, between the two men, that Carter would go on ahead to Egypt to begin excavations in October of that year.

They had decided to work in an area in the Valley of the Kings, near to the tomb of Ramesses VI, before the main visitor season had begun. It was one of the last grid sections yet to be explored.

Carter arrived in Luxor on Friday, 27th October and began work on 1st November.

Below. Howard Carter's drawing of the excavation sites worked on by the two men, from 1917 to 1921, in the Valley of the Kings.

Courtesy of the Griffiths Institute.

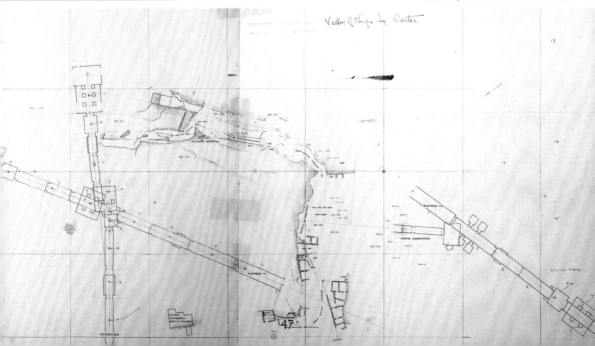

5

The Tomb

Within three days, Carter struck the top step of a sunken staircase some thirteen feet below the level of the tomb of Ramesses VI. Carter telegraphed Lord Carnarvon to come immediately and waited for his arrival. It took Lord Carnarvon and his daughter Evelyn, two and a half weeks to travel from Highclere Castle to Luxor.

Together, the excavators began to clear the stairwell. At the bottom was a full plastered door with seal impressions bearing the name of Tutankhamun.

The door looked as if it had been re-sealed, and nervously the team removed the doorway. Beyond it was a sloping tunnel, part of which had also been refilled.

By 4pm on Sunday November 26th 1922, all the rubble had been removed, the corridor was empty and another plastered door lay in front of Lord Carnarvon and Carter. It was again covered in seals.

Nervously, Carter made a small hole in the door, and reached up to hold a candle. The candle flickered as the air escaped.

The names of Tutankhamun

The Egyptians considered the name of a person or god crucial to their very existence, their role in life and the Afterlife. The name commemorated the person and was a way of gaining power over another being.

Name changes marked important changes in a King's career, hence Tutankhaten changed his name to Tutankhamun, reinstating the importance of the god Amun, who had been obliterated by his predecessor, Akhenaten. Meanwhile, all stelae and monuments created by Akhenaten were comprehensively destroyed and his image erased. A name testified to a person's well being: one punishment to offenders in society was to change their name to one indicating misfortune. The names of the dead needed to be preserved, in order for them to prosper in the Afterlife.

Images, therefore, needed to be named which has allowed Egyptologists to identify paintings and statues and to date them.

The Prenomen - Nebkheprure

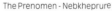

The Nomen - Tutankhamun

Golden Horus Name

The Golden Falcon Name

The Nebti Name

C arter wrote in his
   diary:

"Presently my eyes grew accustomed to
the light, details of the room within
emerged slowly from the mist, strange
animals, statues, gold... everywhere the
glint of gold... for the moment an
eternity... I was struck dumb with
amazement and, when Lord Carnarvon...
enquired anxiously, 'Can you see
anything?'. It was all I could do to get
out the words: 'Yes, wonderful things'.

He then widened the hole, so Carnarvon
and he could see using an electric torch.

Carter tried to describe the exhilaration,
the overwhelming excitement and the
extra-ordinary profusion of grotesque and
unknown beasts carved in gold.

They looked for the coffin and mummy,
but couldn't see it.

Carter had informed Rex Englebach, local Chief Inspector of the Antiquities Department, of the initial discovery of the steps, and that he had witnessed the clearing of debris from the door on Friday, 24th November. Then, after they had breached the second door, sent a note round, explaining that they were going to enter the second door.

On the morning of Monday, 27th November 1922, Howard Carter, Lord Carnarvon, Lady Evelyn, Arthur Callender and a representative for the Inspectorate, stepped into the first chamber using electric light from the main valley system.

"3,000 - 4,000 years maybe have passed and gone since human feet last trod the floor on which you stand...and yet, the blackened lamp, the fingermark on the freshly painted surface, the farewell garland dropped upon the threshold you feel it might have been yesterday...time is annihilated by little intimate details such as these".

The search of the chamber showed that the door in the wall space between the two guardian figures had been breached before, so thieves of early millenniums may have robbed the inner chamber.

The Chariot

Six chariots were found in the tomb. Two of the chariots were finely decorated and Howard Carter described them as 'state or ceremonial chariots'. Reliefs and mouldings decorated the sides and most of the surface was covered with gold, an awesome sight for Tutankhamun's subjects, or his enemies.

Two other chariots were thought to be lighter, hunting chariots and a further one possibly used for practice and exercise. The sixth chariot was not able to be reconstructed.

Chariots had been introduced into Egypt some 200 to 300 years earlier. They quickly became an essential part of army strategy and were vital in ancient Egypt's success in mobile warfare.

Only one other chariot had ever been found, so the wealth of these chariots was of inestimable value. All the leather harness had rotted away over the intervening time, but gilded wood saddle yokes were found, as well as several blinkers, fly whisks, whip stocks and linen trappings.

Tutankhamun bore the title of Commander in Chief of the Army, but he also probably led at least one battle. His chariots were decorated with bound captives. Given the number of bows and arrows, it would be fair to assume he was well trained in their use and enjoyed sporting pursuits.

Twelve chariot wheels were found in the antechamber. They were made from wood and then bound in leather. Each wheel has six spokes which would have been joined to the axle. They had been dismantled before being brought into the tomb.

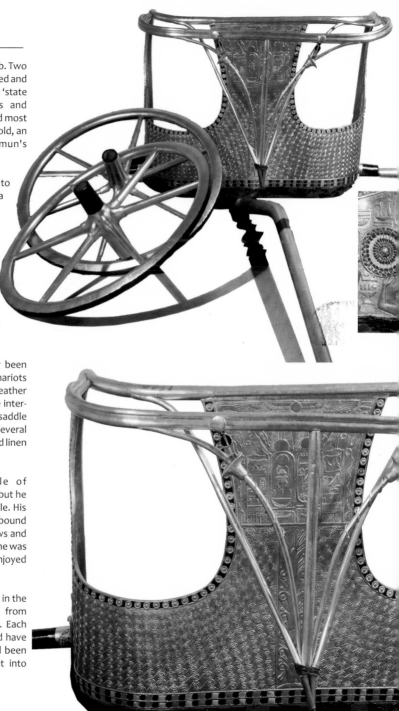

Hathor Bed

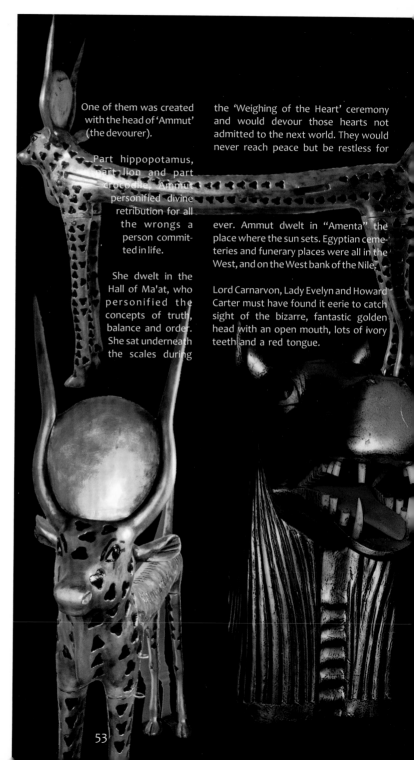

A pair of elongated Hathor (cow) figures form the sides of the bed with a woven mattress between them. Two other gilded couches filled the sides of the antechamber when Carter and Carnarvon first peered into the room.

Magnificent yet very unfamiliar, such beds were only known from wall paintings. They were probably magical and symbolic rather than actual beds upon which the King would have slept. One of the Egyptian myths tells of how the goddess Hathor became the sky itself as she flew towards heaven.

They helped Tutankhamun pass into the next world. Each bed was inscribed with his name. The short dedicatory text on the Hathor bed reads:

'May the good god live, may he be one who loves for ever, namely the Lord of the Low Lands who holds the sovereignty of Re, the Osiris King of Upper Egypt Nebkheprure, true of voice, beloved of Isis Mehet'.

The reason for the combination of animals and gods can only be deduced from partial texts and paintings. Two other ritual couches were found in the antechamber.

One of them was created with the head of 'Ammut' (the devourer).

Part hippopotamus, part lion and part crocodile, Ammut personified divine retribution for all the wrongs a person committed in life.

She dwelt in the Hall of Ma'at, who personified the concepts of truth, balance and order. She sat underneath the scales during the 'Weighing of the Heart' ceremony and would devour those hearts not admitted to the next world. They would never reach peace but be restless for ever. Ammut dwelt in "Amenta" the place where the sun sets. Egyptian cemeteries and funerary places were all in the West, and on the West bank of the Nile.

Lord Carnarvon, Lady Evelyn and Howard Carter must have found it eerie to catch sight of the bizarre, fantastic golden head with an open mouth, lots of ivory teeth and a red tongue.

Guardian Statues

The principal figures representing Tutankhamun were placed either side of the entrance to his Shrine: 'strange and imposing figures'.

They were indeed life size - about 5'6' (1.67m) high, placed on pedestals and adorned with headdresses, so they seemed even taller and more awesome. They were and are very dramatic figures, dominating the first room.

One of the Egyptian religious beliefs was that the spirit needed a body in which to live in the next world, so he would be provided with spirit statues. The Guardian statues were exactly the same height as Tutankhamun.

An eight layer collar lies around the neck of each statue with a breastplate decorated with a scarab. Like the mask and other representations, the ear lobes were pierced. Tutankhamun's kilts were different to those of his subjects. They were starched and ornate.

Each statue holds a staff and a mace, part of the ceremonial regalia. The staff and mace were symbols with which to protect from and smite the King's enemies as they guarded his tomb.

Tutankhamun's statue body was painted in thick black paint and the apparel, faces and decorative details were all gilded. A buckle of the belt holding the kilt in place is inscribed and bears the King's cartouche.

The kilts bear an inscription giving the name of Tutankhamun: 'The good God of whom one may be proud, the Sovereign

of whom one boasts, the Royal 'Ka' of Horakhty, Osiris, King Lord of the two Lands, Nebkheprure'.

Each statue is slightly different, one wearing the 'nemes' head cloth and the other wears the 'afnet' head cloth representing the 'ka', the spirit of Tutankhamun. The 'ka' was his ever present spirit from birth which now joins Tutankhamun in death.

The black colour with which much of the statue was painted, was associated with

regeneration, perhaps because of the fertile black soil of Egypt. The Pharaonic Egyptians called their land 'kemi', the black land.

Three other examples of statues, such as these, are now in the British Museum in London and came from the tombs of Ramesses I and Ramesses II.

oxes and Baskets

tankhamun was sent forth into the
xt world with an ample and wide
riety of provisions.

e white egg shaped boxes contained
nts from goats, sheep, cows, duck and
rious geese.

ver a hundred baskets were found
roughout the tomb. Some were oval,
hers round and a few bottle shaped.
ey might have contained seeds, hops,
rries, fruit, bread and garlic. Fruits of
e dom palm and nab fruit buried with
tankhamun are still sold in the markets
Luxor today.

The Fan and the Shield

The handle of the fan is decorated with a scene showing Tutankhamun driving his chariot whilst out hunting.

One side of the fan shows him shooting two birds with his dog bounding along beside him. The dog then retrieves the two birds. It is a scene of action.

The other side shows a more sedate return with his two attendants carrying the birds. The horses' bridles are decorated with plumes and sun discs and their harness rugs are obviously also richly decorated.

It is a picture rich in detail, from how Tutankhamun controlled his horses, to the wrist guard he wore, the spare bows in the case strapped to the inside of the chariot and the looped reins on the prancing horses, as he returns in a more leisurely fashion. The birds are likely to have been ostriches, which existed in Egypt until 150 years ago.

This type of fan would have been used in royal and religious processions. It originally had 15 white and 15 brown feathers arranged alternately, but they disintegrated over the millennia to leave just the gilded wood.

Three different shields were found: one depicts Tutankhamun seated on his throne, another with him as a sphinx, and lastly as the king slaying lions.

The one at Highclere shows the Pharaoh seated on a throne surrounded by symbols of Kingship showing the unity of Egypt. He is holding a crook and a flail and a sun disk is set above his head.

he Golden Bird

gilded statue of the falcon 'Gehemsu'. is shown here in a mummified form pporting a flail from its back. Blue glass used for the eyes and markings whilst e beak is made from black glass.

he text on the base records tankhamun who is beloved of Sodpu, ho was also described as 'Lord of the reign countries'.

 with new statues and concepts, we n only surmise some 3,500 years later, at perhaps this divine bird is offering otection to Tutankhamun at the edge the Egyptian Empire.

Figure of Netjer-ankh

This fine carving of a cobra was found in its own wooden shrine, which also held the falcon 'Gehemsu'. The wood was gilded, and the eyes set in bronze.

The rearing figure of the cobra was associated with the sun god and Lower Egypt. It appears many times in the tomb, on Tutankhamun's diadem, on his coffins and on a pendant on his mummy. Part of Tutakahmun's name was the Nebty name.

The text on the plinth reads:

*'Osiris Nebkheprure beloved
of Netjer-ankh'.*

6

The Secret Doorway

Above. Lord Carnarvon, left, and How
Carter, right, commencing the demoli
of the doorway to the Shrine Room

On 17th February 1923, Lord Carnarvon and Howard Carter stood on a small platform in front of their distinguished guests and began to knock through the secret wall into a space beyond.

As they began to pull out the first blocks in the small, humid tomb, they began to see the great golden wall of the first Shrine.

Carnarvon and Carter climbed carefully down into the burial chamber which was completely occupied by the first huge Golden Shrine. The walls had been painted yellow with various scenes from the myths progressing Tutankhamun from this world to the next.

Later on, they found it was the first of four Shrines, nested around the sarcophagus. The Shrines were a tight fit, which suggests that the artists and craftsmen had to concentrate on the most important elements and the most important wall paintings.

Above. The entrance to the Shrine Roo
of the tomb, flanked by the two guardia
statues

e Shrines represent the Royal soul's
ssage through the four Worlds of
eation: Manu (Water), Aakhut (Fire),
stau (Earth), and Ament (Air).

ch Shrine, constructed of gilded oak, is
ignificently inscribed with scenes and
erary passages from the sacred books,
ich disclose the spells needed to enter
ese worlds and acquire the powers which
ide there.

ile the Shrines embody the cosmologi-
dimension of the tomb, they also
mbolise the regional traditions of
yptian territory in their architectural
atures.

e Shrine represented here at Highclere
stle (the smallest and first to enclose the
ne sarcophagus) is modeled after the
ehistoric Shrine of the North, with a
rrel-vaulted roof between two vertical
lls. It was a tight fit around the sarcopha-
s.

e Shrine depicts the Deities most closely
sociated with protecting the King after
ath and taking care of his organs, which
ere mummified and placed in the
nopic jars and then in the Canopic chest.

scribed on the walls of this Shrine is
apter 17 of 'The Book of Going Forth
Day', the mystical text of hymns
d spells found in various versions
d lengths in both temples and
mbs.

e design evokes the ancient his-
ry of Egypt and the long line of
tankhamun's predecessors. They
lived in the image of the King, just
the legacy of Osiris lived in his son
rus, the prototypical Ruler of the Two
nds.

Left. The seal to the Shrine door

This innermost Shrine is 9 ft (2.90m) by
nearly 5ft (1.48m) Each of the shrines
reflected a symmetry of ratios as they
fitted one inside another.

The ratio of length to width was two
for each Shrine and the height fell in
similarly harmonious proportions.

The seal depicts Anubis over nine
bound Nubians with the cartouche of
Nebkheprure at the very top.

Wall Paintings

Round the walls surrounding the Shrines were a series of four wall paintings. All four of them are represented here at Highclere. They depict scenes from the ancient Egyptian 'Book of the Dead'.

This was a series of spells and hymns to allow the deceased to take part in the Afterlife. They were magical texts and were often accompanied by illustrations.

The texts and vignettes were written on linen, vellum or papyrus and they were also found on the walls of tombs and on coffins. Their purpose was to provide for and to protect the deceased.

The walls were prepared with a thick layer of plaster and then painted an ochre colour with a horizontal black line defining the area just below the ceiling. The line finishes in each corner with a pointed black tip, the hieroglyphic symbol for eternity.

The North Wall

The North Wall of the burial chamber shows Tutankhamun's successor, Ay, performing the opening of the mouth ceremony for Tutankhamun, who appears here as Osiris, Lord of the Underworld. Ay is cloaked in a cheetah skin facing the boy King, who is depicted in a white shroud, the colour associated with mourning. Ay's name is inscribed over his figure.

The following figure to the left is again Tutankhamun, but now living, and he is greeted by the goddess Nut. Finally, he and his spirit, his Ka, are welcomed a embraced by Osiris, King of t Underworld, with whom Tutankham becomes one. The figures are gen touching and welcoming each other kind, friendly gestures that are recogr ably compassionate 3,500 years later

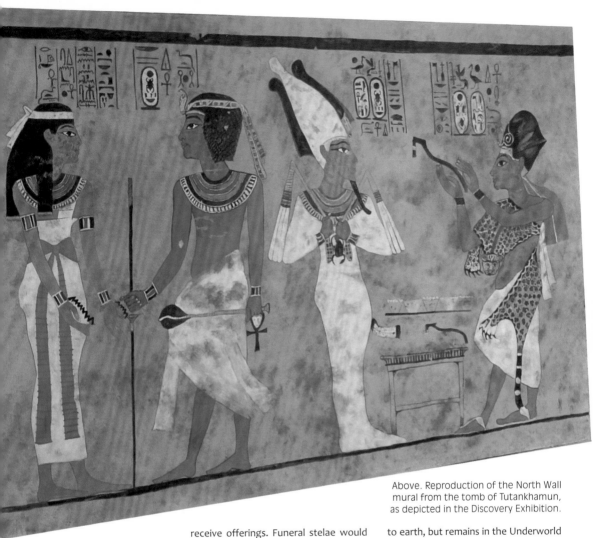

Above. Reproduction of the North Wall
mural from the tomb of Tutankhamun,
as depicted in the Discovery Exhibition.

ne Egyptians believed that you would
ave this world to live, hopefully, with
he blessed dead' (the 'akh'). One of the
ost commonly mentioned forms of the
uman spirit was called the 'Ka', which
eemed to represent a spiritual body, but
so the innate vital energy of a human
eing. The 'Ka' existed both in life and
eath.

fter death, the deceased could also be
ranted the 'ba'. Symbolised as a bird, it
ould temporarily return to earth to

receive offerings. Funeral stelae would
ask for the 'ba' to: 'go forth, to re-enter
the tomb '.

Osiris is the crucial figure in the travel to,
as well as the existence in, the Afterlife.
He appears the most often and other
gods become his cohorts. The myth of
Osiris can be summarized as follows:

Osiris, the son of Nut and Geb, rules Egypt
at the very beginning. He is murdered by
his jealous brother Seth and dismem-
bered. Isis gathers the scattered parts
together and reassembles him. Although
he has been resurrected, he cannot come

to earth, but remains in the Underworld
with his right of Kingship passing to his
son, Horus.

He is always depicted in a mummiform
costume with his head and hands free. He
may also be given the attributes of
Kingship in some paintings, with a crown,
flail and crook.

After death, the different parts of the
deceased's personality will be brought
together and become transfigured to an
enlightened spirit, the 'akh'.

The South Wall

The South Wall of the burial chamber is partly damaged, because Carnarvon and Carter had entered through it from the antechamber. It was a central part of the ritual of resurrection.

sents the god Anubis and is reaching out to touch Tutankhamun, as if in approval.

Behind Anubis stands Isis, to welcome the Pharaoh to the Kingdom of the Dead.

The ritual allowed the mummy to e[...] breathe, see, hear and enjoy the off[...] ings and provisions performed by [...] priests and officiants, thus to sustain t[...] 'Ka' during the spirit ceremony.

It portrayed the symbolic animation of the mummy by magically opening its mouth, so that it could breathe and speak. There is evidence of this ritual from 3,000BC to the Roman period.

Tutankhamun is simply dressed in a loin cloth with a 'khat' headdress. The goddess, Hathor, is facing him and gently touching his mouth with an 'ankh', the symbol of life.

Standing behind the boy King is a priest wearing a jackal-headed mask. He repre-

Above the figure of Tutankhamun, in the white headdress, the hieroglyphic writing ask for him to be given eternal life.

Special tools were used to perform the 'Opening of the Mouth Ceremony'. These included a ritual adze (woodworking blade), an arm shaped ritual censer, a forked blade known as a 'peseshkaf', a serpent-head blade, and a variety of other amulets. A calf's leg was also held up to the lips painted on the coffin.

The Egyptians believed that from t[...] time of a person's death until the perf[...] mance of this ceremony, the body cou[...] not hear, see, or speak. Once the cer[...] mony was finished, the use of the sens[...] returned and the deceased could eat a[...] drink in the Afterlife.

After the ceremony, an offering of foo[...] ointment and clothing was given to th[...] deceased.

The West Wall

The West Wall of Tutankhamun's tomb is, perhaps, the most important. It illustrates an extract taken from the old royal funerary text, the 'Book of Amduat', which records what happens in the Underworld.

The two upper panels show five Deities preceding the solar barque, and one shows Tutankhamun in the image of Osiris. The panels below depict twelve baboons representing the first twelve hours of the night through which Tutankhamun must travel before rebirth at dawn. His journey starts in the west and ends with the newborn sun in the east.

Baboons became associated with a number of the most important Egyptian gods, as well as with the King, and had an important role in ancient Egyptian religion. Baboons and monkeys obviously display human characteristics and were imbued with mysterious and mystical rituals.

Like other Deities, they symbolised good and bad aspects and, in fact, the image of a baboon with raised tail serves as the hieroglyph for 'enraged'.

There were no native monkeys or baboons in Egypt in the New Kingdom. They were probably imported from Nubia. They may have been kept as pets, but baboons were also held in colonies by the priests in the temples, as were other animals that were associated with the gods.

The god Thoth was associated with the moon and was represented by a baboon. The moon was used to calculate time and fractions, so Thoth also became the god of knowledge.

At the moment of death, we all leave the familiar to face non-existence or chaos on the trail that takes us to the next world. The Egyptians recognized it as a perilous time but, with the help of their gods, each mortal could face the trials which the gods had faced already.

Osiris, for example, was not exempt from struggle. The forces of chaos were consigned to the fringes of their world on earth and in the Afterlife. The images present a serene and calm affirmation of the next life.

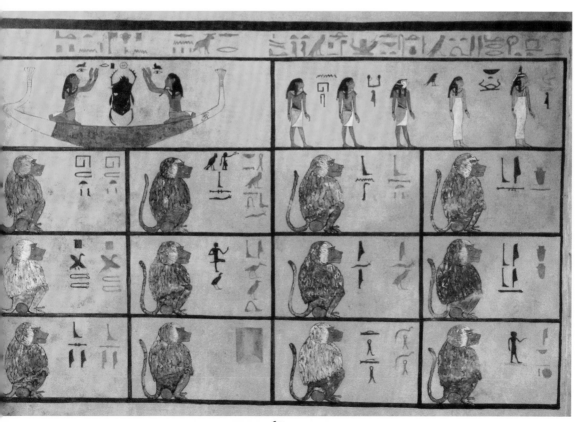

The East Wall

The East Wall of the burial chamber illustrates the death and official earthly mourning of Tutankhamun. He lies in a beautifully canopied bed depicted as the mummified Osiris. The shrine is crowned with two rows of friezes of cobras wearing the sun disc. Isis and Nepthys sit on the bow and prow of the boat watching over Tutankhamun.

The boat itself is on a sled, which is being pulled by five groups of men, dressed in white (the colour of mourning) with white headscarves. Two mourners are distinguished by their shaven heads and could possibly be the viziers for Upper and Lower Egypt, Pentu and Usermont. The inscription above their head describes them as high officials of the palace.

They speak in one voice saying 'Nebkheprure come in peace of God, Protector of the Land'.

The Egyptians tended to provide and plan their burials well in advance. The coffin, tomb and decorations were often made well before the owner's death. It would have been even more important for the Pharaoh to plan and equip his tomb, as well as building a mortuary temple.

By the time of Tutankhamun, this would have been a separate place from the tomb.

The necropolis and the tomb were juncture between this world and t next. A successful burial and resurrecti into the next world required a prop treatment of the mummy, correct bur procedures, a ritual opening of t mouth ceremony and offerings for t spirit afterwards.

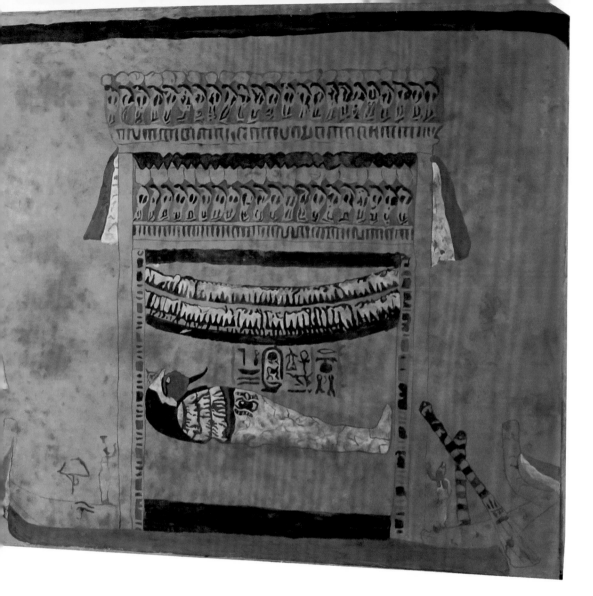

the centre of the Egyptian's world is ̣ flat oval earth surrounded by oceans. ̣ gods come into being and seem to ̣et at the horizon. The '*akhet*' is some-̣es written with an oval determinative. 's is connected to the word '*akh*', ̣ich means the soul like state of the ̣ssed dead.

̣e sky was an important place in the ̣smology of the Afterlife. It held the sun and stars, and also the heavenly bodies associated with the gods and deceased mortals. It was traversed in the Afterlife, usually by boat. The goddess Nut person-ified the sky.

Underneath the earth, was the counter-part to the sky, the abyss the '*Nun*' or primordial waters. It was the origin for the forces of chaos. As in many aspects of Egyptian beliefs, negative forces had some positive sides to them. One part of the legend was that the sun entered the waters every night and emerged at dawn as the newborn sun, Khepri.

As well as the '*Nun*', there was a vast region called the '*Duat*', which was the abode of many of the Deities, including the ones that caused chaos and posed a threat.

The Second Coffin

The King's embalmed body was found inside three golden coffins. They were made from wood which was overlaid with a sheet of gold. This second coffin, however, was then intricately decorated with inlays of different coloured glass and semi precious stones. The decorative motif is called 'rishi' (feather pattern).

On each of the three coffin Tutankhamun's arms are crossed in fro of him holding the two symbols Kingship, the crook and the flail.

Beneath the crossed arms, the Egypti artists incorporated into the feath pattern the outline of a vulture and cobra, each holding in each claw a 'she ring.

The vulture was associated with a nu ber of female deities and the hieroglypl symbol of the vulture (pronounc 'mwt') also means mother. It was al the symbol for the goddess Mut. T German word for mother ('mutter') markedly similar.

e symbols of Upper and Lower Egypt ecorate his headpiece: the '*Wadjet*', the bra of lower Egypt and '*Nekhbet*', the lture of Upper Egypt.

e plaited beard is associated with the d Osiris.

e physiognomy of the face suggest it ay have been made for someone else, t used in a hurry for Tutankhamun.

The foot of this coffin (and of the other two coffins), is decorated with a carving of the goddess, Isis.

It is a very beautiful work of art, perfectly fitting the shape of the end of the coffin, and reflecting again the intricate feathers and '*rishi*' pattern of the lid of the King's coffin. She is kneeling on the hieroglyph sign for gold.

The Mummy

The mummy of Tutankhamun was the first undisturbed Royal Mummy ever found.

It lay in the centre of four gilded shrines and four coffins. The innermost coffin was made from solid gold.

When found, the mummy was not in particularly good condition. It had probably been doused with various unguents before sealing, so some moisture had been trapped in the coffins.

The skeleton clearly showed that Tutankhamun had died between 18 and 20 years old, as only part of his femur had fused. Part of the bone around the hip had still not united with the epiphysis and the arm bones confirmed the same age range.

The various autopsies have confirmed that Tutankhamun was a lightly framed young man about 5'5 or 5'6 tall, which is also the height of the guardian statues.

Howard Carter and his team faced tremendous difficulties as they tried to extract the mummy from the coffin. They used various hot knives to free the body from its wrappings.

Tutankhamun's body was again examined in 1968 led by Professor Harris and, lastly, in January 2005, led by Dr. Zahi Hawass.

Howard Carter's notes list well over 100 pieces of jewellery decoration and amulets positioned and bandaged around the mummy. They were all to help transform the King from death into the new life. They lay from top to toe along the mummy and especially around the neck.

The mummy here is shown with several pectoral collars, bracelets, a dagger, a cobra and four large gold circlets with a T-shaped amulet lying on top. Each toe was encased in gold within the gold sandals. It meant that Tutankhamun would defi-nitely have feet to walk with, even if t[he] mummification of his toes was not qui[te] perfect.

The amulets were a kind of protecti[ve] magic. Magic had many more positi[ve] connotations than it does today when it is seen as superstition. The most common word for magic was the 'heka' and Coptic equivalent mageia then was used in the New Testament from which the word 'Magi' is used every Christmas.

The basic meaning is a mouth and it is closely associated with the power of speech. Thought, speech and deed can all be united in the idea of 'heka'. Endowed with magic, you could make words and desires effective.

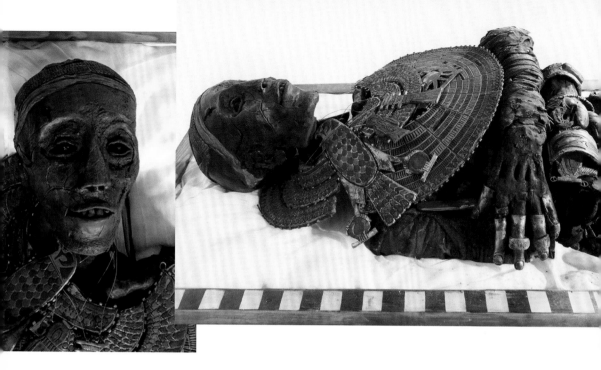

Protective amulets on the mummy were especially important because the mummy might not be in a position actively to defend itself.

Many of the scarabs and amulets were green in colour, made from a type of stone called nephrite. The Egyptian word for green meant to flourish, which also suggests the revitalisation which would happen in the Afterlife.

Interestingly, many of the necklaces of the figures in the wall paintings of the burial chamber incorporate the theme of green nephrite and the face of Osiris is also green , which was also consistent with illustrations in the 'Book of the Dead'.

The heart was the only organ left inside the body and the 'Book of the Dead' devoted several chapters to its preservation and protection. As an additional back up several heart amulets were wrapped up with Tutankhamun's mummy.

The heart was used to represent the person and all their emotions and deeds when it was weighed against the feather at the judgement of the dead.

The Golden Mask

This is one of the most famous images in the world.

It is magnificent, evoking both the tragic boy King and the extraordinary craftsmanship of the Egyptians at that time.

The burnished gold mask is made from two sheets of solid gold and was placed over the linen bandages wrapping Tutankhamun's mummy. It is an extraordinary portrait of a boy laid inside the tomb in 1325BC.

The gold is of equal thickness throughout the work of art except over the left cheek where it is slightly thinner. It weighs 11kg.

The collar across the chest has twelve rows of beads, made up of semi-precious stones and glass. The 'nemes' headdress is made from burnished gold inlaid with blue glass.

Like the coffins, the headdress of the mask bears the two protective symbols on Tutankhamun's brow: the vulture 'Nekhbet' and the cobra 'Wadjet', both made from solid gold.

Similar to all the other representations of the boy King, the ear lobes of the mask are pierced, although covered with gold discs when found.

A falcon's head lies on the shoulders inlaid with obsidian and glass.

Yet, it is the face and the eyes which mak the Mask a personal portrait of a boy wh became a Pharaoh.

The Mask Inscriptions

The back of the mask is inscribed with spells to protect the various parts of the mask. They had been used for over 500 years and invoke each of the individual gods:

'Your right eye is the night bark [of the sun god],

your left eye is the day bark,

your eyebrows are [those of] the Ennead of the Gods,

your forehead is [that of] Anubis,

the nape of your neck is [that of] Horus,

your locks of hair are [those of] Ptah-Soker.

[You are] in front of the Osiris [Tutankhamun], he sees thanks to you,

you guide him to the goodly ways,

you smite for him the confederates of Seth so that he may overthrow your

enemies before the Ennead of the Gods in the great Castle of the Prince, which

is in Heliopolis...the Osiris, the King of Upper Egypt Nepkheprure, deceased,

given life like Ra.'

The Canopic Chest

During the 4th Dynasty, the Egyptians sought to preserve the internal organs of the deceased by storing them in Canopic jars.

The lids of these jars represented the four sons of Horus. Each son would protect a different organ:

> Imsety: the liver and gall bladder,
> Hapy: the lungs,
> Dutemef: the stomach,
> Qehnesenuf: the intestines.

Canopic chests were made from either limestone or alabaster. Tutankhamun's Canopic chest is beautifully carved and very different from its predecessors 1,500 years earlier.

It was protected inside its own golden shrine with an exceptionally beautiful figure of a slender goddess, extending her arms to guard the precious contents of the Shrine.

The chest is carved from one block of alabaster. A separate lid was found covered in a piece of linen. The same four slender goddesses are carved around the corners of the chest: Isis, Nepthys, Neith and Selkis.

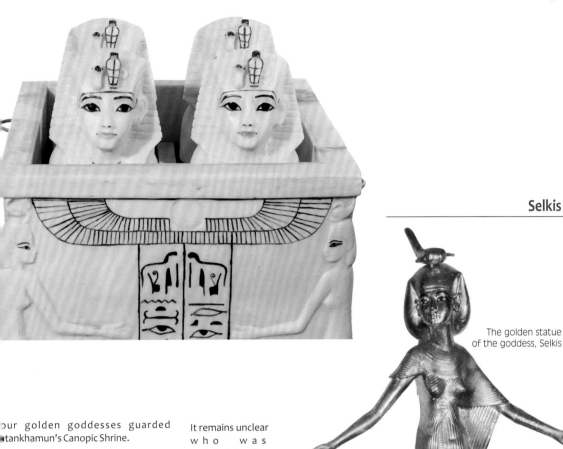

The golden statue
of the goddess, Selkis

our golden goddesses guarded tankhamun's Canopic Shrine.

ach slender goddess faces slightly to the ft or right protectively reaching out her rms to enfold the parts of tankhmaun's body. Each is identified y her headdress: Isis bears a seat, Neith vo arrows, Nepthys a basket and Selkis ight), a scorpion.

ach goddess is portrayed in what is alled the 'Amarna style', that of tankhamun's predecessor, with a oftly protruding stomach and hips hich probably suggests fertility. Just e goddess's eyed are outlined dramati- ally in black.

heir outstretched arms are still touch- gly protective today, 3,000 years later. is and Neith, however, invoke the oodwill of Qehnesenuf and Imsety.

It remains unclear who was sculpted in the Canopic stop- pers. (See above).

They might be a representation of the gods, or they may have been adapted to represent the Pharaoh Tutankhamun himself.

The outer Golden Shrine was decorated with a double row of friezes of cobras. It then opened to reveal the inner alabas- ter canopic shrine which was protected again by the same carved goddesses.

Inside the alabaster Shrine were four exquisite solid gold coffins inlaid with precious stones and glass. They held the King's liver, stomach, lungs and intestines.

73

7

The Golden Throne

Lord Carnarvon described the Golden Throne as 'one of the most marvellous pieces of furniture that has ever been discovered'. Included in our 'Treasury', this beautiful and richly decorated piece was actually found by Lord Carnarvon and Howard Carter under a piece of black linen in the antechamber.

It is a work of art that illustrates the transition from the 'Amarna' religion of Tutankhamun's predecessor, Akhenaten, and the re-introduction of the traditional religion and rituals of post and pre Amarna.

The centre of attention is the scene on the chair back: Tutankhamun and his wife, Ankhesenamun, under the rays of the sun, the Aten. Scenes such as this have been found at Tutankhamun's boyhood home city, Tell el-Amarna, (where Carter worked in his early days in Egypt) and in works of art from Akhenaten's period.

Dressed in silver on a background of gold, Tutankhamun's wife Ankhesenamun is gently anointing him with oil. It is an intimate family scene.

Their names were later changed to reflect the re-introduced religion worshipping the 'Amun'. So, the cartouches read Tutankhamun instead of the original Tutankhaten and Ankhesenamun rather than Ankhesenpaaten.

he rays of the 'Aten', or sun disc, repre-ent the monotheistic religion of khenaten, Tutankhamun's father. herefore, this Throne was probably rought with Tutankhamun from his alace at Tell el-Amarna to Thebes.

The Throne is made from wood, covered in sheets of gold and decorated with glass, faience and semi precious stones. Missing from the throne

were the struts underneath the seat, which probably contained jewels and, therefore, would have been a target for early robbers of the tomb.

The Painted Box

f all the extraordinary pieces of art nd golden treasures discovered by ord Carnarvon and Howard Carter, he "painted box" was most admired. he detailed scenes are painted in empura on a gesso base and show cenes from Tutankhamun's life and eign.

ne side shows him in battle gainst the Syrians; another shows utankhamun defeating an army of ubians; the lid shows him hunting. ach end illustrates the Royal artouches and symbols of Royalty. is executed in intricate and skilled etail.

utankhamun drives his fiery horses nto battle, with Nubians collapsing n a confused mass under his feet. lis fan bearers follow him and founded warriors fall under his hariot whilst others are taken risoner.

arnarvon and Carter took the hest into Seti's tomb nearby. They vere using this tomb as a estoration laboratory. It took early 3 weeks to empty the casket. n the top were a pair of rush and apyrus sandals, then a gilt eadrest, a mass of linen clothes and robe covered in beadwork. Many of he chests had obviously been re-

packed in a jumbled way. Howard Carter could only surmise that originally the chests must have been carefully packed with a purpose. The tomb contained over 50 boxes, most of which

had been ransacked by robbers; so, today, we can only guess that they held clothing and personal treasures for the next world.

The Sailing Boat

Thirty five boats were found in the tomb, reflecting both their symbolic importance and their regular everyday use. Living by the Nile, boats were central to the Egyptians' life and a fundamental part of their religious beliefs.

Tutankhamun might wish, in the next world, to enjoy majestic tours or pleasure trips, on barges and sailing boats, or skiffs for sailing amongst the reeds. The boats were beautifully carved, with one or two oars, cabins, elaborate masts and sails. However, most of the linen sails had disintegrated.

Many of the boats were found in disarray in the Treasury, although they were found still pointing westwards like other undisturbed boats.

Over seventeen of the boats had been thrown in a jumble into the annexe. They were needed in the Afterlife and the Pharaoh used the solar barques to accompany Re (the Sun God) on his journey across the sky.

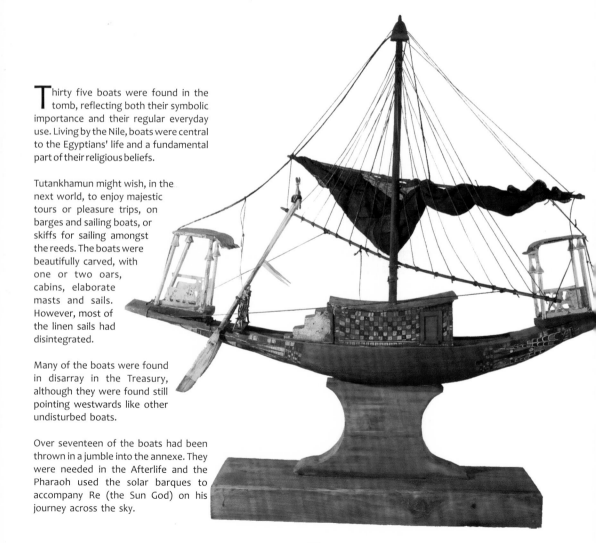

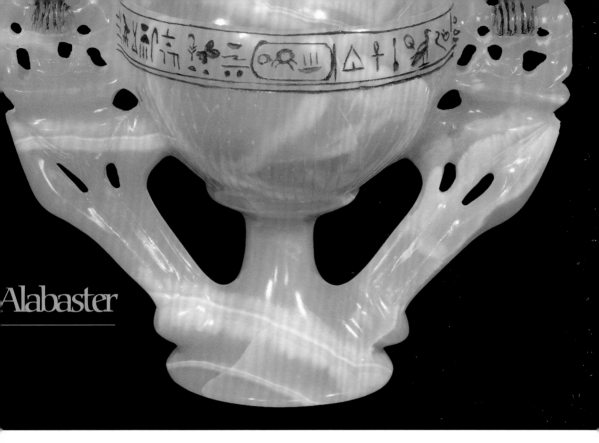

Alabaster

he Lotus Chalice

ord Carnarvon and Howard Carter ⸱und this alabaster chalice lying on the ɔor. Perhaps it had been dropped as ⸱bbers escaped from the tomb in ⸱cient times.

is shaped as a Lotus flower with two ⸱ricately carved handles supporting a ⸱sket and statue of 'Heh' (the god of ⸱ernity) holding an 'ankh' in each hand.

The hieroglyphs around the rim of the cup incorporate Tutankhamun's cartouche with his names and titles in life and then the wish:

'may your Ka live, may you pass millions of years you who love Thebes sitting with your face towards the north wind and your two eyes seeing happiness'.

This inscription can also be found on Howard Carter's gravestone in Putney Vale Cemetery, south west London. (See the panel in the Castle Egyptology Exhibition, Middle Chamber).

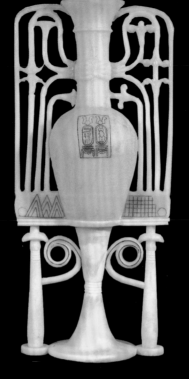

Alabaster Vessels

Above left.
Perfume Vase

It is carved from alabaster, a calcite mineral which name may be derived from the ancient Egyptian word 'alabaste' (vessel of the Egyptian goddess Bast). Alternatively, it has been suggested that the name was derived from the town of Alabastron (near Tell el-Amarna in Middle Egypt).

Oils and unguents were highly valued by the ancient Egyptians. As with the other vases, the robbers had emptied out the oil, but left the vase above.

Above centre.
Perfume Vase with papyrus columns

The stems of the papyrus plant create the handles and the stand of this elegant perfume vase.

The grouping of the openwork design at the bottom suggest the rings of eternity. The centre again bears the cartouche of Tutankhamun.

Above right.
Lamp with painted scene

This delicately carved and painted lam shows Tutankhamun (identified by h cartouches) sitting on a throne wearing blue crown. He is about to be dresse with a lotus garland by his wif Ankhesenamun. The scene was painte on a calcite insert and is a remarkab example of ancient Egyptian craftsma ship.

The lamp is flanked by handles carve with the figure of the god 'Heh', suppor ing Tutankhamun's cartouche and a 'ankh' as the symbol for eternal life.

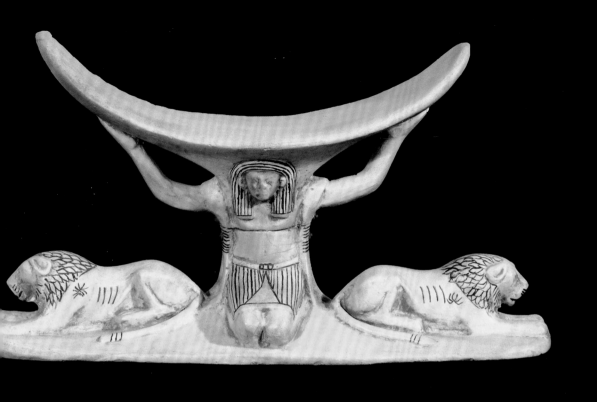

Ivory Head Rest

ght headrests were found throughout
e tomb. They would have been covered
th linen to provide support during
ep. They were beautifully made and
e ivory headrest is quite unique. The
d 'Shu' kneels to support the curved
adrest, flanked by two lions looking to
e eastern and western horizons. The
ck of the pillar bears a column of
eroglyphs with Tutankhamun's
rtouche. Reading down the column:

*'The Good God, son of Amun, King of
pper and Lower Egypt, Lord of the two
nds Nebkheprure, given life like 'Re' for
ever'.*

cording to Egyptian myth, 'Shu'
ought order out of the chaos and
eated the Universe by raising the sky
gh above the earth. However, he al-
ays has to carry on supporting it.

Tutankhamun's dummy

Underneath the great ritual couches in
the antechamber, Howard Carter and
Lord Carnarvon found a most unusual
piece, a torso of Tutankhamun. Nothing
like this has ever been found in other
tombs. Carter suggested it could be a
mannequin used for tailoring clothes.

It is made from wood and painted with a
Royal uraeus on the forehead. The ear-
lobes are pierced and the crown is a
simple plain shape on which, perhaps,
headdresses or diadems could be tried .

An enormous amount of garments,
however, had been packed. Ceremonial
outfits, tunics robes, shirts, coats, head
cloths, shawls, gloves, caps, shoes, (over
90 pairs of sandals or shoes), and much
of it was decorated with beadwork, gold
sequins or embroidery.

Ihy

The Statue of Ihy

This painted black figure was stored in a shrine box with two figures of Tutankhamun as a harpooner and one of Tutankhamun wearing the red crown.

The figure is not identified by any inscription, but is thought to be the child god Ihy, carrying a gilded sistrum (a musical instrument) in his right hand. His hair is worn long in a side lock and the statue is made from wood, blackened with bitumen, whilst the eyes and sistrum are gilded.

Sekhmet

A Child's Chair

Six chairs were found in the tomb with foot rests and other stools. The golden throne was obviously the most sumptuous and prestigious, but others were beautifully carved and elegant.

The small ebony chair was probably made for Tutankhamun when he was a child. It is likely that the ebony came from the Sudan.

The legs are shaped like lion claws, inlaid with ivory. The back support is decorated with inlaid ivory. The inside arm panels, however, are made from gilded wood decorated with desert plants, whilst an ibex decorates the outside.

The other wood used to create some of the furniture was cedar - most likely from Lebanon. It was a much prized wood and was used to make the two ships, for example, that were found buried in the sands by the Giza pyramids.

The Statue of Sekhm

Many gilded divine figures we found in the tomb. The statue Sekhmet the 'powerful on was found in a shrine shap chest in the Treasury. The so disc on her head indicates h Royal status. She was asso ated with the Sun God, Ra.

She was originally the warri goddess of Upper Egypt and depicted as a lioness, a therefore a fierce hunter. S was seen as the protector the King and a leading figure warfare. It was said that h breath created the desert.

She was a very acti goddess, stalking the lan bringing justice through t avenging of wrongs.

Her principle centre worship was at Memphis, b countless statues in her ima; have been found througho Egypt.

ilver Trumpet

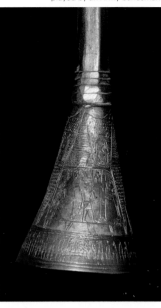

Visitors to the Castle Egyptology Exhibition can hear the 1939 recording of the trumpet being played by an Army bandsman.

o trumpets were found in a corner of the rial Chamber. One was made from beaten ver with a rolled mouthpiece of gold, and the her from copper or bronze, overlaid with ld. The one displayed here is based on the ger silver trumpet.

ly three trumpets have survived from the yptians times. Wall paintings suggest trumts were used to encourage military success.

o sistra and a pair of clappers were also found the tomb. Both trumpets were found with a corated wooden core which would have lped keep the soft metal in shape when not in e.

e silver trumpet is engraved using shapes of tus blossom, sepals and flowers, with vertical rtouches containing Tutankhamun's me. The bell of the bronze trumpet shows its rpose clearly: it is decorated with the figures Re-Horakhty (the falcon god), Amon-Re,

Tutankhamun and then Ptah (in a mummified form). These three gods are associated with the army so it suggests a military use for the trumpet. Tutankhamun is wearing the blue crown, the 'khepresh', also called the war crown. It was a tall helmet, adorned with golden discs, with the uraeus and vulture on the brow.

The famous battle scenes inscribed on the temple at Medinet Habu in Thebes, show Ramesses III wearing the blue crown of war, a trumpeter by his side.

They are powerful instruments, used to rouse and encourage and were probably used in battle. It is not very long so would have produced the limited range of notes you can hear on the recording taken from the original instrument.

The silver trumpet was played in 1939 by an English army bandsman when it suffered some damage, but has since been repaired.

he Diadem

1e Diadem was found underneath the olden Mask around the head of tankhamun. The vulture and uraeus ead were detached and placed on the ighs of Tutankhamun's mummy.

1e gold band is inlaid with circular eces of carnelian. The circular motif is flected in the golden pendant ribbons hich extend down at the back.

oward Carter noted how beautifully arved the vulture's head was. He said it as a particular type of vulture. He loved 1e birds of the desert and had spent uch time drawing them. It was hinged fit over different headdresses.

8 The Vault

Anubis, the Jackal

The old vault at Highclere Castle contains three figures: a Guardian Statue, Anubis, the Jackal and Hathor, the cow. The Guardian Statue is described in this book in the Wonderful Things section, page 54.

The tomb's Treasury was dominated by the magnificent large statue of the jackal God, Anubis. He is sitting on a Shrine, with carrying poles running under the mounts. He was covered by a red linen shawl.

The corniced Shrine is made of gilded wood and Anubis is carved with silver toe nails and jewels for eyes. It is a very elegant animal with a long, lean, lithe body and narrow face.

Anubis was the god of embalming and, therefore, quite properly guarded the Canopic Shrine. He is quite a menacing figure and, perhaps, his haunting statue put off robbers from raiding the Treasury. The Shrine itself contained various compartments with amulets and jewellery.

The Shrine itself is decorated with 'djed' and 'tyet' signs. The 'djed' sign was associated with stability. The 'tyet' sign can be translated as life or welfare.

The Head of Hathor

This magnificent head was partly gilded and partly covered in thick black resin. The horns were shaped in wood and then covered with copper sheets.

Hathor was one of the most widely worshipped goddesses throughout Egypt.

She combined the idea of Motherly love, represented by the cow suckling her calf, and the fury of a mother defending her young.

The Minor Pharaoh

The 18th Dynasty marked a golden era in Pharaonic history. The Egyptians had established control over their bordering lands, requiring treasure in tribute. The country was rich in gold, had fertile soil and, therefore, had developed sophisticated art and culture.

Much of the wealth was retained by the Pharaoh, but a large proportion went to the priesthood and temples. As in European medieval history, it must have lead to confrontation and competition.

Akhenaten, the probable father of Tutankhamun, emphasised the Aten (Sun disc), which was a monotheistic cult or religion, stemming only from the Pharaoh Akhenaten. In order to create the new religion, he built palaces at Tell el-Amarna away from Thebes. He commissioned many new statues and altered previous art and temples.

This art was distinctive and more stylised. In some ways, the extended heads of the Pharaonic family reflect and incorporate the royal headdresses into the actual head of the Pharaohs.

Tutankhaten became Pharaoh at 9 years of age. Initially, he lived at Tell el-Amarna, in his father's great new temple and palace. Three years later, he was crowned at Thebes and his name became Tutankhamun.

The real power in the land lay with A Master of the Horse, who was al related to Tutankhamun. Administratic was centred at Memphis, so he possib also spent time there. The priests and c gods were reinstated and co-existe alongside the Aten god.

Tutankhamun lived in a palace at Theb built by Amenophis III, his grandfathe completing monuments his grandfath had started.

His fame today is probably due to the fa that he died young, was hastily buried ir small inconspicuous tomb and did n have the time to play a major part in th history of the 18th Dynasty.

Ay succeeded Tutankhamun for a sho time, before Tutankhamun's gener. Horemheb, became Pharaoh and rule for the following 28 years.

Lotus Head

One of the most unusual pieces is this wood sculpted head of Tutankhamun. It was actually found buried in the rubble in the corridor leading to the tomb. Perhaps it was a small piece that early robbers had thought about taking but dropped, as of little value.

It was the subject of some controversy when, it was discovered in 1924, packed in some wine cases. The Egyptian authorities immediately accused Carter of intending to steal it. Nor had he originally recorded it...

The sculpture represents Tutankhamun as Nefertum, (the beautiful or youthful

Atum). The young Atum rose from t primeval waters, (the Nun) at th Creation of the World and the birth Life.

He was supposed to have risen in the bu of a blue water lily, so he is associate with this flower. He rose with the su and was associated with sunrise. Some the titles are 'He who is beautiful' 'Water Lily of the Sun'. He was ofte carried as a good luck charm.

The sculpture has the elongated he associated with Akhenaten's reign, so may have been made at Tell el-Amarr and brought with Tutankhamun Thebes, when the court moved back ar Tell el-Amarna was abandoned.

The King as Harpooner

...his outstanding statue was found in the ...easury. It is a beautiful and sensitively ...rved statue, capturing Tutankhamun ...st as he is about to throw the weapon.

...e is balanced on a skiff and is holding a ...pe, which would have been attached to ...e harpoon. It is made from wood and ...ded in gold. Tutankhamun wears the ...d crown of Lower Egypt.

...oward Carter wrote:

'The statuettes of the King show the influence of the El Amarna school in the modelling of these particular figures ... even though they be of the traditional type there is a direct and spontaneous feeling for nature ... they show both energy and grace ... in fact the divine and the human have been brought in familiar touch with one another'.

Bow Fronted Travelling Chest

The tomb contained over 50 chests and boxes. They were in all shapes and sizes, from long trunks to small jewellery boxes. Some were roughly made, but many were beautifully finished.

One of the most unusual was the bow fronted chest. It was made using two layers, a stout frame with thin wooden boards covered by fine ebony and hardwood. The layers of wood cross-line each other creating a sturdy structure. There are few clues to what it originally contained. The hieroglyphic inscriptions are simply the names of Tutankhamun and Ankhesenamun. Howard Carter noted that there are a few messy pieces of linen and clothing plus an hieratic docket.

This box was found on top of the Hathor bed in the antechamber and the detachable lid in the annexe. It is such a usefully made secure box that it may well have been much used in life by Tutankhamun and simply buried with him. It might have been used to hold papyrus rolls. It is made from veneered wood and bears the cartouches of Tutankhamun and Ankhesenamun.

Shabti

Shabtis were the figures who would carry out manual duties in the next world. Royal burials, such as that of Tutankhamun, included many examples of beautifully carved figures, some carrying the hoes, flails and baskets they might need.

The Egyptian hieroglyph translates as: 'rw nw prtm hrw'. 'Rw' is the word for mouth or thing said, 'nw' genitive plural of 'of', 'prt' is a verb to arise, 'm' a proposition for 'in', 'hrw' is the word for day.

'Coming Forth by Day', Spell 6 of 'The Book Of The Dead' instructs the Shabti as follows:

O Shabti, If 'the deceased' be summoned to do any work which has to be done in the realm of the dead,
to make arable the field, to irrigate the land or to convey sand from East to West, 'Here I Am', you shall say,
'I Shall Do It'.

413 Shabtis were found i Tutankhamun's tomb. They were most stored in black painted boxes. 176 were the Treasury, 236 in the Annexe and escapee in the antechamber.

They were carved in a variety materials, some were in wood with bla painted details, others were who gilded, further ones were made faience or calcite. Most of the figures a represented wearing Royal headdresse

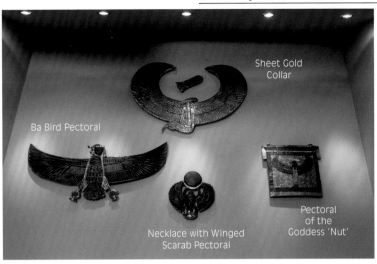

Sheet Gold Collar

Ba Bird Pectoral

Necklace with Winged Scarab Pectoral

Pectoral of the Goddess 'Nut'

Necklace with winged scarab pectoral

The central part of the necklace spells out Tutankhamun's Prenomen, the hieroglyphic signs for Neb-KheperRe. But, on this pendant, the disc representing the sun is also supported by a crescent moon. This was often the way that the god Osiris was depicted. The scarab has been given finely detailed and jewelled wings made from lapis lazuli, a green glass and carnelian. It was found with a golden chain, but may have had other fastenings originally, which suggests that Tutankhamun wore this piece of jewellery whilst he was Pharaoh.

Sheet Gold collar

This fine gold ornament was probably made for Tutankhamun's burial. It lay across his chest. It had been thinly beaten and then carved to show the cobra 'Wadjet' throwing protective wings around the Mummy of the King.

Pectoral of the Goddess 'Nut'

This piece of jewellery was found in the Shrine of Anubis and the jewelled border suggests the shape of a shrine. Nut (the sky goddess) stands in the centre spreading her arms and wings protectively around the cartouches of Tutankhamun.

Ba Bird pectoral

This pectoral also lay on Tutankhamun's Mummy. It depicts an open winged falcon with the head of a man. This represents his 'Ba', the spirit whowould come into being after death and reanimate the deceased, allowing him to take on other forms. The falcon remained a powerful symbol throughout Egyptian civilisation.

The hieroglyph of a falcon came to stand for 'god'. It was associated with a number of Deities but the primary association was with Horus. Here, therefore, all the symbolism is woven together in different layers.

The claws hold the 'shen' ring which is the sign of eternity. The wings are intricately inset with coloured glass. Tutankhamun's head is turned to the right , is beautifully carved and wears a diadem of similar shape to the one found in his coffin.

different crowns and Royal symbols and insignia.

Each shabti is, however, a work of art in its own right. They are often beautiful pieces of sculpture, each with a different expressive face.

10

Death

Lord Carnarvon
Team

From Treasure to Tragedy

Lord Carnarvon left for London to re-quest all possible help from experts from the Metropolitan Museum of New York, to consult the British Museum and to discuss how best to handle the world press. Howard Carter travelled to Cairo to acquire the practical supplies they needed such as wrappings, secure gates and chemical supplies.

With Howard Carter's approval, Lord Carnarvon signed a media contract with the London Times. The media and public interest was overwhelming. Lord Carnarvon hoped to deal simply with one press outlet, who would then dissemi-nate the news to all other worldwide newspapers. Instead of decreasing the excavator's stress, it actually made the whole situation worse with jealousy and continual sniping. It drove other newspa-pers into frenzied efforts to get round the agreement.

(Above, left to right:) Arthur Mace of th Metropolitan Museum, Carnarvon's Privat Secretary Richard Bethell, Arthu Callender, Lady Evelyn Herbert, Howar Carter, 5th Earl of Carnarvon, chemis Alfred Lucas of the Egyptian governmen and official photographer Harry Burton.

Lord Carnarvon and Howard Carter realised that they had discovered a King's tomb which surpassed their hopes and dreams. With hindsight, their challenging trials on the road to its discovery were the easier part of the journey. Who, in fact, owned the tomb and its contents? Who would publicise it? Who would control the next stage?

They quickly realised that they would need to assemble the best team in the world to record, document, photograph, preserve and manage the excavation. It had become a world event.

Howard Carter and Lord Carnarvon argued about the degree of public access as the first room was cleared. Carter became increasingly fraught and intoler-ant of the constant interruptions. There were a great number of people in a very small space.

Lord Carnarvon's health was inherently poor and he was stressed and exhausted.

Recuperating on a dahabayah on th Nile, he was bitten by a mosquito. He ha returned to Cairo in March 1923 to dis cuss, with the Egyptian government, th details of his excavation. Lord Carnarvo still owned the concession to excavate i the Valley of the Kings. The director o the Antiquities Department was Frenchman, Pierre Lacau, and the gov ernment posts were shared between th British, the Egyptians and the French.

However, Lord Carnarvon suffered fron recurring high fevers and was bein nursed by his daughter Evelyn. Howar Carter rushed to Cairo to be with him. Hi wife flew out from England and nurse him night and day. He fought to live and each day his health was reported aroun the world. However, he died from pneumonia brought on by septaecemi on April 5th 1923.

Guests arriving for the 'Official Opening' of the Tomb

tomb. In the end he seemed to feel disenchanted. He wrote that, after all the years working to clear and record the contents of the tomb, he knew as little about the Pharaoh Tutankhamun at the end of his excavation, as he had at the beginning.

Yet, the contents of the tomb are personal and do provide an outstanding insight into the loves and life of the King. They shed light on life, art and religion. Any of the works of art found in the tomb are outstanding in their own right and show the exquisite skills of Egyptian craftsmen, sculptors and artists.

Tutankhamun's gold mask has been a symbol for the Pharaonic civilisation which spanned some 4,000 years, magnificent yet personal. He sought resurrection and the Afterlife through a properly constructed tomb and hoped, through his behaviour and values, to be accepted into the peace of the next world, rather than consigned to the restlessness of the Underworld.

He died too young and, just like Lord Carnarvon, before he had fulfilled his role in life.

Lord Carnarvon and Howard Carter's discovery has incalculably increased our knowledge about this fascinating civilisation, its beliefs, way of life and art.

Lord Carnarvon fought so hard to live, he died knowing there was so much to do, a personal tragedy. Nevertheless, his endeavour and persistence had added immeasurably to the world's

utankhamun's small crowded tomb in he Valley of the Kings yielded 5,398 eparate items, from magnificent hrines to simple pottery, games and oys, chariots, boats and trumpets. Some f the items are the only actual examples ve have today of the workmanship and onstruction of practical items only therwise known from paintings or apyrus scrolls. Historians have searched or clues about his reign and the history f that period.

oward Carter spent five years after the eath of Lord Carnarvon clearing the

knowledge of the ancient Egypt of some 3,500 years ago.

Tutankhamun was consigned to anonymity and eternal life for some 3,500 years and has now achieved a different sort of eternal fame.

Above. Visit of the Queen of the Belgians. Below left. Lord Carnarvon, Lady Evelyn Herbert, Howard Carter. Below. Lord Carnarvon resting at 'Castle Carter'.

DEATH OF LORD CARNARVO

FATAL ILLNESS FOLLOWS MOSQUITO BITE

EARL'S FAME AS EGYPTOLOGIST : SPORTSMAN AND MANY-SIDED M

TO BE BURIED ON THE TOP OF BEACON HI

IT is with the deepest regret that we have to record the death of the Earl of Carnarvon, High Steward of the Borough of Newbury, which took place at Cairo at two o'clock on Thursday morning. When the "Newbury Weekly News" went to press at midnight on Wednesday, the latest telegraphic news available was that his lordship had made a gallant rally, and there were some faint hopes of recovery. But as Egyptian time is two hours fast on Greenwich, the end was approaching. The family, including Lady Carnarvon, Lord Porchester and Lady Evelyn Herbert, were gathered around the bedside. Consciousness was maintained until the final passing.

The sad news was received in Newbury on Thursday morning with the greatest regret, and the flags at the Municipal Buildings and Parish Church were hoisted half-mast high. By his own wish the late Earl is to be buried at the top of Beacon Hill.

The House of Eternity

The contents of Tutankhamun's tomb tell us how he lived, yet many writers have spent most of their time asking how he died.

Did he die in suspicious circumstances or was it of natural causes? Television documentaries and books have suggested he died from a blow to the back of his head because of unusual X-rays of his skull.

More recent analysis with the benefit of CT scans and advanced medical technology have suggested that he had broken his leg just below the knee, perhaps as a result of a chariot accident. Gangrene would have set in and most likely been the cause of his death. Apart from that, his health would appear to have been good and he led a busy life.

His tomb was not very large and, whilst he was buried with due procedure, it was also hurried. A coffin was adapted for his tomb and beloved toys and games hurriedly assembled for his funeral.

It may have been robbed twice of small items and unguents (very valuable in antiquity) within a short time. Then, his memory was thoroughly obliterated as Egypt moved on to grandiose building schemes with Tutankhamun being completely forgotten. A rock fall near Ramesses VI tomb would have protected it further from disturbance over the millennia.

Present day forensic investigation has indicated that Tutankhamun may have died in January or February. The preparations for his funeral would then have taken about 70 days. He may well have been placed in his tomb at the end of March or beginning of April, a time eerily convergent with the time of Carnarvon's death.

Lord Carnarvon and Tutankhamun were each buried in the Spring, each chose lonely awe-inspiring burials, one in an arid desert foothill, the other on a wind-swept bleak Iron Age hill fort. Each died from the effects of septaecemia.

LORD CARNARVON'S LAST MOMENTS.
The "Times" Cairo correspondent gives an account of Lord Carnarvon's illness and last moments.

After the closing of the tomb of Tutankhamen at the end of February, Lord Carnarvon and Lady Evelyn Herbert went for a change to Assuan and they returned to Luxor on March 6th. Two days afterwards, while he was up the Valley of the Kings, Lord Carnarvon was bitten on the right cheek—by a mosquito it is believed. He paid no attention to the bite, and in shaving took off the scab. The minute exposed wound became infected, possibly by dust, but more probably by a fly, and a slight swelling showed itself in one of the glands. Medical aid was sought at Luxor, and when he left for Cairo on March 14th, he was decidedly better.

At Cairo, however, Lord Carnarvon suddenly became worse and on the 17th erysipelas and steptococcis blood poisoning of the head and neck developed. As soon as the germ had been identified and the necessary culture made he was given a serum injection, which was promptly effective. His temperature, however, ran high during the next few days, and he was in great pain, as the inflammation affected the nasal passages and the eyes. He was, in fact, in a very serious condition, and Lady Carnarvon was summoned from England, and Lord Porchester from India, but by the time Lady Carnarvon arrived on March 26th the poisoning had, for all practical purposes, disappeared. Unfortunately, on the next day, pneumonia of the right lung set in and the patient's condition again gave rise to much anxiety. Again and again he rallied and when Lord Porchester arrived on April 1st his condition was quite hopeful. On the 2nd, however, the left lung became infected, and he had to be kept going with oxygen stimulants. His condition got steadily worse and on the 3rd it looked as if he would not live through the night.

Next morning, however, Lord Carnarvon made another wonderful rally. The temperature dropped and he seemed to have taken a turn for the better and called for a barber to shave him. Throughout the day the improvement continued and every one went to bed in a frame of mind which was as optimistic as it had been pessimistic twenty-four hours before. About midnight he was not so well. Again he seemed to pick up, but at about 2.30 a.m. he was seized with a violent fit of coughing, which ranged him much distress. Medical aid was immediately at hand, but his heart could no longer stand the strain, and five minutes later he passed away peacefully, in the presence of his family, whom fortunately there had been time to summon. The body was transferred to hospital for embalming before being brought to England for burial at Highclere.

TO BE BURIED ON BEACON HILL.
We are able officially to announce that at Lord Carnarvon's special request he will be buried on the top of Beacon Hill. The exact spot has not yet been fixed, but it will be right at the summit, within the British Encampment. The wish is an original ...

from Newbury. On its bold summit are the distinct remains of a British campment. The ancient entrenchment the flat summit is in fine preservation ditch is well preserved and very d About a mile south-east of Beacon Hill Seven Barrows, or Tumuli. Some of were opened many years ago, and found to contain burnt bones and ash From its isolated position the hill is a inently fitted for a Beacon, and has pe ably been so used from the earliest tim Doubtless here flamed forth one of thousand twinkling points of fire, stretch in an endless range, which heralded Armada's coming, and which Macau celebrated with his most sonorous rhetor when:—

From Eddystone to Berwick bounds, fro Lynn to Milford Bay,
That time of slumber was as bright, busy as the day.

There have been celebrated beacon fir there in more recent years. There was o the occasion of Queen Victoria's Jubile 1887, again on King George's Coronatic Day in June, 1911, whilst the last wa July, 1919, upon the occa...

THE LATE LORD CARNARVON

Outside Tutankhamen's Tomb. With him is Lady Evelyn Herbert, who was present at the discovery, and Mr. Howard Carter.

[By kind permission of "The Times."]

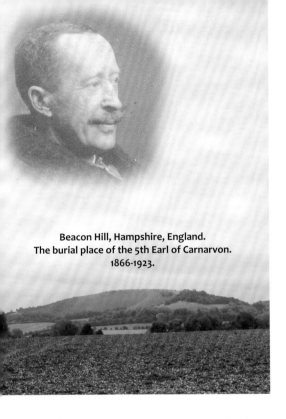

Beacon Hill, Hampshire, England.
The burial place of the 5th Earl of Carnarvon.
1866-1923.

Pyramid Mountain, East Valley of the Kings, Thebes, Egypt.
The burial place of the boy Pharaoh, Tutankhamun.
1344BC-1325BC.

fter the 5th Earl's death, Queen
lexandra wrote to Lady Carnarvon:

*'I offer you and your family heartfelt
sympathy with the terrible sorrow you
have sustained in the death of your
husband, whose name will be
remembered with pride by his
fellow countrymen'.*

ing George and Queen Mary wrote:

*'The Queen and I have learnt with deep
regret of the death of your father especially after the splendid fight which he
made for his life. We offer you and your
dear mother and family our sincere
sympathy in your great loss'.*

oward Carter and the late Earl's widow
vere left to deal with the thorny subject
f the Carnarvon concession and the
ontrol over the excavation. The follow-
ng years were marked by legal disputes.
Nevertheless, Lady Carnarvon continued

to pay for the costs of the excavation,
until it was finally completed some years
later. It took a further four years to complete the conservation of the objects.

At a time of rising Egyptian nationalism
and intense interest in the tomb, Lord
Carnarvon's Estate lost the right to
continue the concession when Carter
stormed out of the tomb refusing to
work in insupportable conditions. Under
the terms of the concession, Lord
Carnarvon had a right to some or all of
the items in the tomb, depending on
whether it had been disturbed or left
intact. The rest would remain in Cairo.

Lord Carnarvon had written that he felt
strongly that Tutankhamun should
remain in peace in his coffin in his tomb in
the Valley of the Kings.

Howard Carter found relationships with
Egyptian officials, the media and the
public very difficult to deal with, without

his alter ego, Lord Carnarvon. He dog-
gedly completed the task, yet was never
given the recognition and honour he
deserved. He seemed to feel out-
manouvered by journalists and other
conventional experts.

He died on 2nd March 1939. Carter's
funeral later that month, just before the
coming War, was a poor occasion for a
man who had been a national hero during
the previous decade. Only a few people
attended the ceremony at Putney Vale
Cemetery in south west London, including Lady Evelyn Beauchamp (neé
Herbert). and Howard Carter's niece
Phyllis Walker.

**Despite the lack of honour or
recognition to either man, Lord
Carnarvon and Howard Carter remain
known to many people and their story
and that of Tutankhamun retains its
excitement and mystique.**

The Dynasties of Ancient Egypt

First Dynasty: 3,100-2,890BC
The first known Pharaoh was Narmer who unified Upper and Lower Egypt. Hieroglyphs were fully developed and first known on the Palermo Stone (a list of early Pharaonic kings).

Second Dynasty: 2,890-2,686BC

Third Dynasty: 2,686-2,613BC
This and the next 3 Dynasties are known as the Old Kingdom. The royal capital was at Memphis and, during this time, the Pharaoh Djoser built the Step pyramid.

Fourth Dynasty: 2,613-2,494BC
This was the age of the pyramids. Khufu, usually considered a tyrannical Pharaoh, built the Great Pyramids at Giza, whilst his descendants built the smaller pyramids.

Fifth Dynasty: 2,494-2,345BC

Sixth Dynasty: 2,345-2,181BC

Seventh/Eighth Dynasty: 2,181-2,125BC
The 7th to the 11th dynasties marked an intermediate period, defined by droughts, famine and the breakdown of the central administration.

Ninth/Tenth Dynasty: 2,160-2,025BC

Eleventh Dynasty: 2,125-1,985BC
Around 2055BC, Mentuhotep II reunited Egypt and thus began the Middle Kingdom. The capital moved first to Thebes, but secondly back towards present day Cairo at Lisht.

Twelfth Dynasty: 1,985-1,795BC
Many rulers from the twelfth Dynasty were successful warriors, traders and built some fine temples, like the temple at Abydos, on the west bank of the Nile near Thebes.

Thirteenth Dynasty: 1,795-1,650BC
From now until the 18th Dynasty, Egypt disintegrated as a nation state and, later, was ruled by *Hyksos* kings and eventually split into separate kingdoms.

Fourteenth Dynasty: 1,750-1,650BC

Fifteenth Dynasty: 1,650-1,550BC

Sixteenth/Seventeenth Dynasty: 1,650-1,550BC

Eighteenth Dynasty: 1,550-1,295BC
The Eighteenth Dynasty was founded by Ahmose I, the brother of Kamose, the last ruler of the Seventeenth Dynasty. Ahmose finished his brother's campaign to expel the hated Hyksos rulers. The 18th Dynasty became Egypt's most prosperous period and marked the high point of its power.

Nineteenth Dynasty: 1,295-1,186BC
This was dominated by the achievements of the Ramesses who extended Egypt's empire around the Mediterranean coast and through Turkey.

Twentieth Dynasty: 1,186-1,069BC
This period began to decline, as the sons and heirs of Ramesses III struggled with each other, coupled with another period of drought and, therefore, famine.

Twenty-First Dynasty: 1,069-945BC
The 21st to the 25th Dynasty are combined as the third intermediate period. They were characterised by in-stability, fractured administration and civil war. Egypt's international power was waning and another tribe, the Assyrians, was becoming dominant.

Twenty-Second Dynasty: 945-715BC

Twenty-Third Dynasty: 818-715BC

Twenty-Fourth Dynasty: 727-715BC

Twenty-Fifth Dynasty: 747-665 BC

Twenty-Sixth Dynasty: 664-525BC
This was the last native Egyptian Dynast

Twenty-Seventh Dynasty: 525-404BC
Egypt was conquered by an expansiv Persian Empire under Cambyses, wh now became Pharaoh.

Twenty-Eighth Dynasty: 404-399BC

Twenty-Ninth Dynasty: 399-380BC

Thirtieth Dynasty: 380-343BC

Persian Kings: 343-322BC

Macedonian Kings: 332-305BC
The previous 100 years had been continuous battle between the Persian and Greeks, and was finally resolved b Alexander the Great, who ushered i centuries of Greek settlement an cultural influence over distant areas.

The Ptolemies: 305-30BC
Ptolemy was one of the seve bodyguards who served as Alexander th Great's generals and deputies. Ptolemy' family ruled Egypt until the Roma Conquest of 30BC, the most famous an successful of whom was Cleopatra.

Octavian: 30BC
The history of Roman Egypt begins with the conquest of Egypt in 30BC b Octavian (the future Emperor Augustus) following the defeat of Marc Antony an Queen Cleopatra in the Battle of Actium Thereafter, Egypt became a province o the Roman Empire.

ities

hmut	Demoness of death, devourer of the heart in 'The Ceremony of the Heart'
hun	Father of The Gods
ubis	The Jackal, God of Embalming
st	Goddess of Ointment, wife of Anubis, cat-head, sister of Horus
s	The dwarf God of Protection
b	Father of Osiris, is the Earth
pocrates	The child God
thor	The cow Goddess of Love, Music and Beauty
h	The God of Eternity
qet	Frog God of Childbirth and Fertility
rus	Son of Osiris
s	Goddess of Motherhood and Fertility. Mother of Horus and one of 4 Goddesses on Canopic chest (Nepthys, Neith, Selkis)
a'at	Goddess of Truth in the Ceremony
ut	Wife of Amun, often depicted as a white vulture
eith	Goddess of War, one of 4 Goddesses on Canopic chest (Isis, Selkis, Nepthys)
epthys	Sister of Isis, one of 4 Goddesses on Canopic chest (Isis, Neith, Selkis)
ut	Mother of Osiris, the Sky-Goddess
siris	Lord of The Underworld and son of Geb and Nut
.	(Ra), The Sun God
khmet	The powerful one, half woman, half lion, lion-headed
lkis	Goddess of Healing, shown as a scorpion, one of 4 Goddesses on Canopic chest (Isis, Neith, Nepthys)
u	Father of Nut, creates order out of chaos, holds up the sky
bek	The Crocodile God, sat in judgement at 'The Ceremony of The Heart'
dpu	Lord of the foreign countries
oth	Associated with moon, shown as a baboon

inerals

abaster	(Calcite), calcium carbonate
zurite	Deep blue copper mineral
asalt	Black volcanic rock
arnelian	Reddish-brown semi-precious gemstone
olorite	Hard limestone like rock
ience	Blue-green ceramic material
apis lazuli	Blue coloured rock
atron	Natural soda ash
ephrite	Type of green stone
uartzite	Hard sandstone rock
hist	Hard silt stone

bjects

fnet	Type of headcloth worn by tomb sentry statue

Amulet	Wooden models offering protective magic to the Mummy
'Book of Amduat'	A record of the Underworld
'Book of The Dead'	Ancient funerary textbook containing a collection of spells, charms and formulae
Canopic Jar	Containers for embalmed organs
Clappers	Musical instrument like castanets
Dahabaya	Nile sailing boat
Khat	Simple headdress, worn loose
Nemes	Striped headdress, most famously shown on the Death Mask of Tutankhamun
Papyrus	Writing surface made from compressed reeds
Pectoral	Wide jewellery necklace
'Rosetta Stone'	Inscribed basalt stone found by Napoleon's soldiers in 1799
Scarab	Type of beetle found in hieroglyphs
Sesheshet	Egyptian name for sistrum, a musical rattle
Shabti	Wooden or stone models buried in tombs, were workers in the Afterlife
Shen	A shen ring is a circle with a line on its edge, which was used in hieroglyphics as a stylised loop of a rope
Sistrum	A musical rattle
Stela	Inscribed surface made from wood or stone containing hieroglyphs

Pharoahs

Ahmose	(Nebpehtyre) 1539 - 1514 BC, first Pharaoh of 18th Dynasty
Akhenaten	Amenhotep IV / Akhenaten 1350 - 1334BC, 10th Pharaoh of 18th Dynasty, father of Tutankhamun
Amenophis	Amenhotep III (Nebmaatre) 1382 - 1344BC, 9th Pharaoh of 18th Dynasty, grandfather of Tutankhamun
Ankhesenamun	Wife of Tutankhamun
Ay	(Kheperkheperure) 1325 - 1321BC, 13th Pharaoh of 18th Dynasty, succeeded Tutankhamun
Hatshepsut	(Maatkare) 1473 - 1458 BC, 5th Pharaoh of 18th Dynasty
Horembheb	(Djeserkheperure) 1323 - 1295BC, 14th and last Pharaoh of 18th Dynasty, succeeded Ay
Kamose	(Wadjkheperre), last Pharaoh of 17th Dynasty
Merneptah	1213 - 1203, 4th Pharaoh of 19th Dynasty, succeeded Ramesses II
'Ramesses the Great'	Ramesses II (Usermaatresetepenre) 1279 - 1213 3rd Pharaoh of 19th Dynasty
Seti	Seti II (Userkheperuresetepenre) 1200 - 1194, 6th Pharoah of 19th Dynasty

---

Tiye	Great Royal Wife of Amenophis III

Placenames

Abu Simbel	Site of Ramesses II temple
Abydos	On west bank of Nile near Thebes
Birabi	On west bank of Nile near Thebes, near Valley of The kings
Castle	On west bank of Nile near Thebes,
Carter	house built by Carnarvon for Carter
Dra' abu	On west bank of Nile near Thebes,
El-Naga	near to Valley of the kings
Karnak	On east bank of Nile, north of Luxor
Kemi	Ancient Egyptian name for their land, derived from its black soil
Luxor	Modern name for ancient Thebes
Nubia	Ancient name for Sudan
Sheikh abd el-Gurneh	On west bank of Nile near Thebes
Tell el-Amarna	On east bank of Nile, half way between Cairo and Luxor
Tell el-Balamun	Nile delta site north of Cairo
Thebes	Ancient name for modern day Luxor
Valley of The Kings	One of several valleys on west bank of Nile near Luxor

Symbols

Akh	The blessed dead, enlightened spirit, in the realm of the Afterworld, akh was the deceased who became an effective being
Akhet	The place where the Sun rises and sets, often translated as 'horizon'
Ankh	The symbol of Life
Aten	Sun God
Ceremony of The Heart	The removal of the deceased heart and comparison with a feather
Djed	Symbol associated with Stability
Duat	Region in Underworld
Heka	Common ancient word for magic
Ka	Form of the human spirit
Magi	Coptic word for magic
Nekhbet	The vulture symbol found on head-dresses with the Wadjet cobra
Nomen	Type of Pharaonic name
Nun	Region in Underworld
Prenomen	Type of Pharaonic name
Rishi	Decorative feather pattern motif
Tyet	Associated with Life or Welfare
Wadjet	The cobra symbol found on head-dresses with the Nekhbet vulture

Special names

Cartouche	Oblong symbol containing a Royal name in hieroglyphic writing
Demotic	Later form of Egyptian writing
Hieratic	Middle form of Egyptian writing
Hieroglyphs	Early form of Egyptian writing

Postscript: the Carnarvon Legacy

LAST WEEK'S
AVERAGE DAILY SALE
457,000
No 63,022

T
Treasure
By Bryan Appleyard

Lord Carnarvon, the grandson of the man who discovered the tomb of Tutankhamun, has unearthed a hoard of Egyptian antiquities hidden for over 60 years in the family's ancestral home.

More than 300 objects, including a wooden face of Tutankhamun's grandfather dating back 3,200 years, have come to light at Highclere Castle in Hampshire. They had lain there since the early 1920s without the present Earl or any of his family knowing they existed.

Lord Carnarvon, who was Lord Porchester until his father died last September, was astonished by the find. "I thought I knew every nook and cranny of the castle," he said. "I was sure I knew Highclere better than anybody else in the world and I was sure there was nothing Egyptian there."

The discovery fills in the remaining gaps of the extraordinary story of the finding of the Tomb of Tutankhamun — the greatest Egyptian find in history — by the fifth Earl and Howard Carter.

All the objects were uncovered in Egypt to them during several archaeological digs in the seasons before their Tutankhamun find in 1922, or bought by Lord Carnarvon to add to his collection. They sent the antiquities back to Highclere at the end of each season.

Documents, letters and the original snapshot albums, also at Highclere, help to reveal a fascinating background to the historical treasures.

They came to light because a memory of a 75-year-old retired butler who had come out of retirement help the new Lord Carnarvon prepare an inventory of the contents of Highclere Castle. The two men went wandering through the huge house together when the seventh Earl commented that they appeared to have completed their task. The butler...

In 19
astor
by the
tomb
Times
treas
exhibit
Museu
Times
reveal
the Cal
tomorro
serializ
betwee
Tutank

Left: face o

T he Discovery of the Tomb of Tutankhamun attracted criticism and admiration from both experts and amateurs. It involved the two archaeologists, Carnarvon and Carter, with their rights and obligations. It also concerned the pride and heritage of the country of Egypt. In addition, the excavators had to deal with both French and English colonial administrations.

Egyptologists throughout Europe and America wished to be involved or would have ideas for better strategies. The Press tended to attack Carnarvon and Carter, in order to try to find a story without reference to "The Times", which was the newspaper which had an exclusive arrangement with Lord Carnarvon.

Since 1922, millions of people have seen Tutankhamun's mask and treasures. They can be regarded only with awe and fascination. Further research into the works of art and objects from the Tomb will yield still more knowledge in the future.

Both Carnarvon and Carter sought to discharge the task that faced them to the best of their abilities. It was an awesome responsibility, given the extraordinary interest and spectacular publicity which followed the Discovery.

They achieved what people for centuries had only dreamt of, or read about in fabled stories. They found the golden tomb, and completed a legendary quest.

The 5th Earl painted by William Carter, artist brother of the Earl's Egyptologist colleague, Howard Carter.

Lord Carnarvon's legacy was establishe by his widow, Almina, in the years imm diately following his death. Using h father's inheritance, she supporte Howard Carter until the Tomb w cleared. Assisted by the best experts the day, the fragile contents of the Ton were preserved as carefully as possib and documented meticulously.

Every legendary tale has to have a cur and this story too, has unexplaine events. The story of Lord Carnarvon death is well known. It gave rise to th myth of the 'Curse of Tutankhamun'.

Five years after the Discovery, Arthu Mace, who assisted Carter in the clea ance of the Tomb, died in Egypt in th same hotel where Lord Carnarvon ha died. Richard Bethell, Carnarvon's p vate secretary, died four months aft the opening of the Tomb, from hea failure.

Lady Evelyn never returned to Egy after her father's death. However, sh visited the Exhibition, 'The Treasures Tutankhamun', at the British Museum London, in 1972. Sadly, she suffered stroke on the steps of the Museum a she left.

TIMES

MARCH 7 1988

30p

to Tutankhamun found

seum, speaking of the significance of
the find, said: "The material from the
tomb of King Tutankhamun's grandfather, Amenophis III, is particularly
important ... In this country we
previously had very little material of
this sort from the Valley of the Kings.

"Howard Carter was one of the first
really modern excavators in Egypt. He
showed an accuracy, care and system
in his work which had been lacking
previously. The fact that many of
these objects can be matched with his
notes and his published works makes
them doubly valuable. It means we
know exactly what they are and where
they came from. From a scholarly
point of view it is very exciting and of
course there is the romance of whole
story."

And Dr Nicholas Reeves, a curator
at the British Museum specializing in
Egyptology, says the finds are very
important and of immense scholarly
value. Many can be identified from
Howard Carter's writings – including,
for example, jewel caskets previously
thought to have been lost forever.

The discovery comes 64 years after
the Carnarvon family was sworn by
the sixth Earl, son of the man who
opened Tutankhamun's tomb, never
again to speak of ancient Egypt. Lord
Carnarvon and his father had never
wanted to talk about Egypt at all. "The
nannies or servants would say he was
frightened of the curse of the
Continued on page 20, col 1

The ferry
grieving
ust end,
vicar

The castle gives up its secret at last: Lord Carnarvon at Highclere with one of the treasures,
an alabaster jar which dates from the 13th century BC. (Photograph: Stephen Markeson)

bove. The 7th Earl is
ont page news in 1988...
elow. The 8th Earl in the
alley of the Kings.

In 1988, the Carnarvon family were again front page news. Throughout the 7th Earl's childhood, he assumed that all of the precious objects from his grandfather's collection had been sold.

Following the death of his father in 1987, he had an enormous surprise when he unblocked the door between the Drawing Room and Smoking Room in the Castle.

It had been closed for many years and, in between the doors, he discovered a series of small pigeonholes in the thickness of the wall. Inside, had been pushed several mysteriously wrapped packages.

Only Robert Taylor, his father's retired butler, had any recollection of what they were: the forgotten finds of the 5th Earl's early expeditions to Egypt. When unwrapped, they proved to be ancient Egyptian artefacts excavated between 1907 and 1920 from the tombs of kings and nobles, and preserved for more than 30 centuries.

With tremendous excitement, the Carnarvon family set off on another treasure hunt, although this time in the Castle. The artefacts discovered were put on display when Highclere Castle first opened its doors to the public.

Now, the 8th Earl has updated and extended the Collection and re-presented the Exhibition in new settings throughout the cellars of the Castle.

Like his great-grandfather, the 8th Earl has become fascinated with ancient Egypt. He has presented TV documentaries around the life and story of the 5th Earl and travelled to many of the 5th Earl's original excavation sites.

The new "Wonderful Things" Exhibition creates a new area of interest for visitors of all ages to the Castle.

Lady Fiona Carnarvon.
8th Countess of Carnarvon

Acknowledgements:
Written by Fiona Carnarvon, with help from Geordie Carnarvon and Duncan MacDougall.

Photography: Highclere Castle attributions: the 5th Earl of Carnarvon, the 8th Earl of Carnarvon, Elizabeth Vickers.

With thanks to Duncan MacDougall for all the work on images and book design.
info@laserprintsoftware.com

With thanks to Ellie Fane for her work on the Exhibition wall paintings.

With thanks to the Griffiths Institute, Oxford; the British Museum, London; 'Country Life' magazine; 'Newbury Weekly News'.

All rights reserved. No part of this publication may be reproduced, stored in a retrieval system, or transmitted in any form or by any means, electronic, mechanical photocopying or otherwise without the prior written permission of the copyright owners. Every effort has been made to fulfil requirements with regard to reproducing copyright material. Any omissions will be rectified at the earliest opportunity.

Highclere Castle has been the ancest family home of the Earls of Carnarvon over 300 years. Today, one hundred ye. after the 5th Earl lived in the Castle, a from which he set off on his expeditic to Egypt, the Castle is still the fam home of the 8th Earl and Countess Carnarvon.

www.highclerecastle.co.uk

Further Reading:
The source material and books consult by the author range from archi material at Highclere, to the Tim Archives, the Griffith Institut biographies of Howard Carter, referen books for aviation, cars, Victorian a Edwardian biographies and varie Egyptian reference works.

© Highclere Enterprises LLP 2013.
Published by Highclere Enterprises L
Printed in the United Kingdom.

For further copies, visit
www.highclerecastle.co.uk

Photo: Highclere Cast